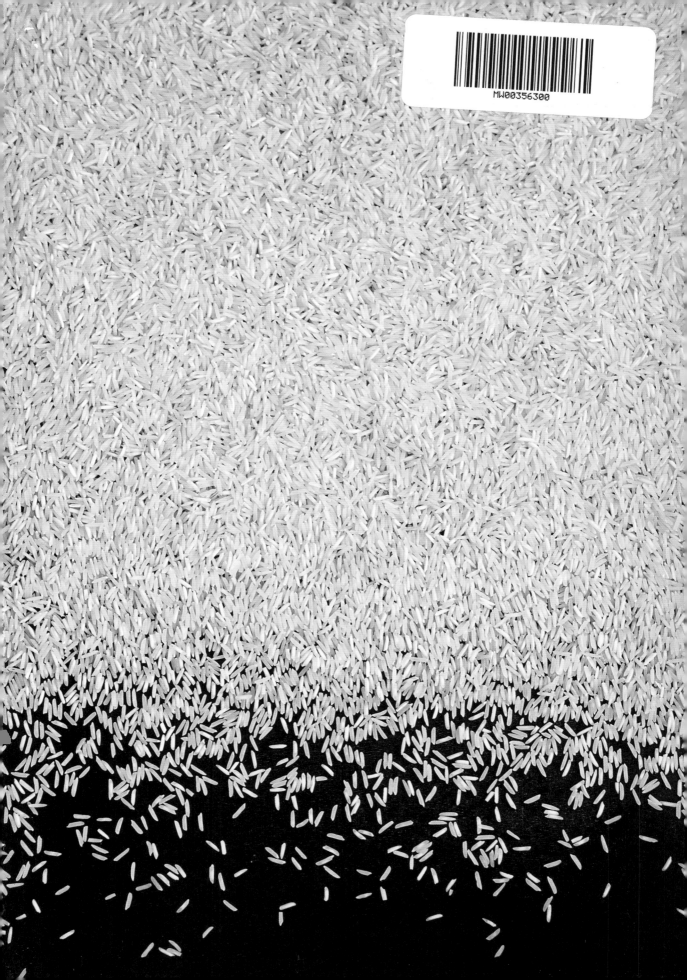

MY indian COOKBOOK

MY *indian* COOKBOOK

AMANDIP UPPAL

PHOTOGRAPHS BY LISA LINDER

weldon**owen**

Contents

Introduction

This book is about discovering a **casual** attitude toward Indian cooking, inspiring an inventive side in experienced cooks and building confidence in others. This is a book that you reach out for, one that holds familiarity and comfort, and one for everyday use whatever the occasion may be.

Stripped back are the regal layers associated with Indian cuisine, making way for a new, informal approach to cooking with Indian spices and ingredients. In this book you will find traditional favorites plus classic dishes from the north and south of India, some of which have been distilled and pared back for busy modern cooks. The recipes continue to hold true to tradition while fitting in with the way you want to cook—preparing ahead where possible and making shopping easy.

My First Indian Cookbook brings Indian cooking **up to date** and will provide you with the basics and inspiration to forge your own path and try something new. Recipes such as Lemon and Saffron Pot Roast Chicken (page 102), Salmon Baked with Crème Fraîche and Coconut (page 104), or Chile Hot Chocolate (page 216) will warm the soul, fire up a love for food, and build an appreciation of spices you may have never even have heard of. These are recipes to celebrate and share communally.

Quick, uncomplicated dishes, with simple steps and helpful tips, will allow you to dip in and out of Indian cooking as and when the mood suits you. It is all about cooking with ease, organization, and simplicity, and guiding you along the way until eventually you feel confident and inspired to use spices in more ways than one.

The love and **appreciation** of good food is a common thread that runs through all the regions of India, central to family life, culture, and pleasure. *My First Indian Cookbook* invites you to join in the experience.

Stars of India

INDIA IS FAMOUS FOR MANY EXCITING REASONS: THE PEOPLE, SPIRITUALITY, AND OF COURSE BOLLYWOOD . . . BUT THE MAIN PULSE AND HEART OF INDIA IS THE FOOD.

DALAI LAMA
His holiness the 14th Dalai Lama
From: Himachal Pradesh
Famous Dishes: Dham, Patande

MAHATMA GANDHI
"Father of the Nation"
From: Gujarat
Famous Dishes: Dhokla, Cilantro and Peanut Chutney, Shrikand

DEEPAK CHOPRA
New Age guru and advocate of alternative medicine
From: Delhi
Famous Dishes: Butter Chicken, Kulfi

RAVI SHANKAR
World-famous classical sitar player and composer
From: Uttar Pradesh
Famous Dishes: Peda, Bharwan Chicken

FREDDIE MERCURY
Flamboyant and eccentric rock star
From: Maharashtra
Famous Dishes: Pav Bhaji, Flaked Rice Poha

ENGLEBERT HUMPERDINCK
An English pop singer and heartthrob
From: Tamil Nadu
Famous Dishes: Idli Sambhar, Masala Dosa

GEORGE ORWELL
Political writer, journalist and novelist
From: Bengal
Famous Dishes: Ilish Paturi, Ras Malai

MIRA NAIR
Accomplished film director, writer, and producer
From: Orissa
Famous Dishes: Crab Kalia, Stuffed Okra

FREIDA PINTO
Most famous for *Slumdog Millionaire* and *Rise of the Planet of the Apes*
From: Goa
Famous Dishes: Prawn Curry, Spicy Sausages

ANUPAM KHER
Mainly a Bollywood actor who has appeared in several hundred films
From: Kashmir
Famous Dishes: Dum Aloo, Yogurt Lamb Curry

AISHWARYA RAI-BACHCHAN
Former Miss World model turned Indian actress
From: Karnataka
Famous Dishes: Beet Curry, Lemon Rice

OM PURI
An Indian actor who has appeared in mainstream commercial Indian and British films
From: Punjab
Famous Dishes: Dhal Makhani, Chicken and Paneer Tikka

Pantry

WHOLE SPICES

Each pungent and aromatic spice can hold its own, or spices can be mixed and matched to create your own unique blends of masala.

AJWAIN (CAROM) SEED
Also known as lovage, this seed certainly has a distinct, piquant flavor. It is mainly used in vegetables, pickles, and breads.

BAY LEAVES
These leaves are frequently used in rice and meat dishes, but are also delicious in dhals and vegetables.

CARAWAY SEEDS
This versatile seed releases a very aromatic, sharp, and nutty flavor. Add to bread, meat, and fish dishes for extra character.

CARDAMOM, BLACK
The aroma and flavor of black cardamom is quite different from green cardamom. It has a distinct smoky, minty coolness to its flavor.

CARDAMOM, GREEN
Second to black pepper, cardamom is one of the most popular spices in the world. It works beautifully in milky desserts or savory curries.

CASSIA OR CINNAMON STICKS
Cassia comes from cassia bark and is related to "true cinnamon." Cinnamon sticks can also be used for the same spicy, sweet flavor. Use ground cinnamon for additional flavor and deep color.

CLOVES
Cloves can be used whole or ground for a powerful sweet but peppery flavor.

CORIANDER SEEDS
The lemony, sweet seeds of the cilantro plant can be ground, toasted, crushed, or used whole. They are ideal in pickles or ground in curry pastes.

CUMIN SEEDS
This spice is often used whole and added to hot oil, or it can be ground. For a smoky, earthy flavor, toast the seeds first and then grind.

FENNEL SEEDS
Fennel has an aniseed flavor that gives a warm, sweet aroma.

FENUGREEK LEAVES
Known as *kasuri methi*, these dried leaves add a strong, distinctive flavor to a curry. Rub the leaves between your fingers while adding to your dish to release the flavor.

FENUGREEK SEEDS
This small hard seed has a tangy, burnt-sugar flavor, so use only in small quantities.

MACE AND NUTMEG
Both these spices are formed on the same plant; they are quite similar in flavor and are mostly used in meat curries and desserts.

CUMIN SEEDS

COCONUT MILK POWDER

TURMERIC

CARDAMOM PODS

CINNAMON STICKS

STAR ANISE

MUSTARD SEEDS

Mustard seeds come in three colors: yellow, brown, and black. It's the black ones that are most commonly used in Indian cooking and are used only in dhals, pickles, salad dressings, and chutneys—almost never in meat dishes.

NIGELLA SEEDS

Ideally used whole in pickles, curries, breads, and salads, these seeds can be toasted and ground at home.

PANCH PHORAN

Also known as Bengali five spice, this spice blend is used to infuse oil and add wonderful layers of flavor to most dishes. Ready-mixed packets of these seeds are available to buy, but if you can't find them then mix together equal quantities of fenugreek seeds (methi dana), cumin seeds (jeera), aniseed (saunf), black mustard seeds (rai), and onion seeds (kalonji). Store the spice mix in an airtight jar and use as and when it is needed.

PEPPERCORNS, BLACK

The perfect spice and seasoning used in every type of regional cooking—use black peppercorns whole or crushed in meat, vegetable, lentil, and rice dishes.

POPPY SEEDS, WHITE

These add richness to a dish. They can be toasted, ground, and then added to dishes or soaked in hot water and made into a thick paste.

GROUND SPICES

Ideally, try to buy ground spices in small quantities and store in screw-top jars or containers.

CHILE POWDER AND RED PEPPER FLAKES

Chile is an important spice, as it gives a dish that bold blend of heat, fragrance, and flavor. Both equally as hot, but flecks of red pepper flakes look attractive, while the powder is best used during cooking as it also releases color. For a deeper color, Kashmiri chile powder works best. If ground or flaked chiles are too hot for you, then replace with cayenne or freshly ground black pepper.

GARAM MASALA

Each region in India and even every household has its own version of garam masala. A maximum of seven whole spices blended together features in most curries for that aromatic warmth. Store-bought powder is fine, but making your own is also easy (see page 242).

TANDOORI MASALA

A mixture of ground spices specifically used for skewered meats and vegetable dishes cooked in tandoors, or clay ovens. Firm favorites include tikka, butter chicken, or paneer as an alternative.

TURMERIC

Not only does this spice add a beautiful deep, rich color to your dishes, turmeric is also a powerful antioxidant and so an aid to digestion and healing.

SAFFRON

CORIANDER SEEDS

www.topolski.co.uk   TOPOLSKI Produce

MACE FLOWERS

BAY LEAVES

RED PEPPER FLAKES

GARAM MASALA

KIDNEY BEANS

COCONUT OIL

WHITE RICE

CHICKPEAS

MUSTARD SEED OIL

GHEE

OILS AND BUTTER

GHEE
An Indian version of clarified butter, ghee has a high burning point and tastes divine in dishes (see page 234). If you find ghee too rich to cook with, then finish off your dish with a drizzle of this yellow, nutty liquid.

MUSTARD SEED OIL
This oil is a popular one for cooking fish in particular and as a base for pickles. It also has a high cooking point, so is perfect for deep-frying. **NOTE:** Heat this oil until a little smoky, let cool slightly, and then use.

PEANUT OIL
An excellent all-purpose oil that is light and extremely popular in most Asian cuisines.

COCONUT OIL
Another oil that has a high burning point, coconut oil is classified as a "superfood" with amazing health benefits. And it is delicious. Organic raw virgin coconut oil is best.

ESSENCE AND FLAVORING

BLACK SALT
Known as kala namak, this salt has a pinkish color, but once added to salads, chopped fruits, and currries it adds a distinct flavor.

CHAAT MASALA
This is a zingy, tangy, and slightly hot spice mix, which is mainly used as a garnish on salads, snacks, drinks, and sometimes curries.

COCONUT MILK
Coconut milk is great for using in broths, marinades, and gravy-based curries. Fairly similar result as coconut milk powder (below), just saucier.

COCONUT MILK POWDER
A perfect all-rounder for adding a smooth richness to curries, soups, dressing, marinades, and cakes. Unless using in baking, make sure to mix with a little warm water to form a paste before adding.

DRY MANGO POWDER (AMCHOOR)
This sour powder is made from dried green mangoes. It is used mainly in vegetable and bean dishes to add that edge of fruity sourness. If you can't find dry mango powder, then use lemon or lime juice instead.

KEWRA WATER
An extract from the pandanus flower, it is used mainly in meats, rice dishes, drinks, and desserts and is similar to rose water.

POMEGRANATE SEED POWDER (ANARDHANA)
This powder has a tart and tangy flavor and is used mostly in crispy fritters, fried snacks, chutneys, yogurts, and sometimes curries.

ROSE WATER
This is a scented water made with rose petals and is delicious used in desserts, drinks, and savory rice dishes.

SAFFRON
Saffron is an expensive, delicately flavored spice that has an exquisite taste and color. Soak the fine threads in warm milk, water, or stock, and add to sweet or savory dishes and drinks.

DRY GOODS

DRIED MINT
For a further intense minty flavor, add to marinades, dressings, spice mixes, and stuffings.

PUFFED RICE
Usually used in breakfast cereals, snack foods, and popular street foods in India.

SEV
Crispy fine noodles made from chickpea flour—sprinkle them on most snack dishes or enjoy them on their own served with drinks.

BEANS AND LENTILS

Beans and lentils have the advantage of adding bulk to a dish or salad, and they are also a great substitute for a meat-free meal.
NOTE: The longer you cook beans and lentils over low heat and stir, the richer and creamier their texture becomes.

CHICKPEAS

Chickpeas have endless uses, but are mainly added to salads, vegetable curries, and rice and meat dishes.
NOTE: This legume needs to be soaked overnight before using, but good-quality cooked varieties are also available in cans or cartons.

KIDNEY BEANS

This creamy, buttery bean works very well mixed in and cooked with most other legume, vegetable, and meat dishes.
NOTE: This legume needs to be soaked overnight before using, but good-quality cooked varieties are also available in cans or cartons.

MASOOR DHAL

A wonderful and versatile lentil that is happy to be blended with other quick-cooking lentils. It can be used on its own as a simple side dish or to bulk up most soups.

MOONG DHAL

This is a skinned yellow split moong bean. It's very quick to cook and is also delicious as a dry-fried dhal.

PUY LENTILS

Not traditionally used in Indian cooking; however, with their lovely bite and flavor, these little green French lentils blend very well with Indian spices. They are delicious cooked in stock and whole spices and used in salads, mixed into a vegetable curry, or scattered over rice with a crispy onion garnish.

TOOR DHAL

Toor dhal has a unique, mildly nutty flavor. Cook it as a soupy broth or mix in with moong dhal and masoor dhal for more variety in flavor and texture.

URAD DHAL

Also know as black gram, these have a distinct strong earthy taste. They are traditionally used in curries, but also ground into a flour or paste and used to make poppadums and dosas.
NOTE: This lentil needs to be soaked overnight before using, but good-quality cooked varieties are also available in cans or cartons.

FREEZER ESSENTIALS

FRESH GRATED COCONUT

Buy several fresh coconuts, scrape out the flesh, and freeze in individual plastic freezer bags.

CURRY LEAVES

Buy a large batch of these leaves fresh and freeze. Similar to a bay leaf, but only smaller, they release a distinct taste and aroma and are added to rice, curries, chutneys, salads, and pickles. Alternatively, you can use bay leaves.

TAMARIND PULP

Although you can buy jars of tamarind pulp, making your own is very easy and much tastier (see page 228). It can be stored in the refrigerator, but it also freezes very well.

CURRY LEAVES

TAMARIND PULP

MOONG DHAL

GHEE

CHICKPEA FLOUR

15 Must-Have Spices

START BUILDING YOUR BASIC SPICE SHELF WITH THESE 15 ESSENTIAL AND COMMONLY USED SPICES. FOLLOWING IS A PARTIAL LIST OF THE RECIPES IN THIS BOOK IN WHICH THESE FOUNDATIONAL SPICES APPEAR.

1 TURMERIC

Ayurvedic Jamu Tonic Drink (page 214)

Beef and Potato Curry (page 110)

Cauliflower and Peas (page 68)

Classic Lamb Curry (page 100)

Crab Fried Rice (page 148)

South Indian Eggplant Pickle (page 184)

Tarka Dhal with Spinach and Fresh Tomato (page 60)

2 CHILE POWDER/ RED PEPPER FLAKES

Eggplant with Chile and Pomegranate Dressing (page 86)

Bean and Lentil Salad with Garlic and Ginger (page 168)

Kale, Chickpea, Mint, and Preserved Lemon Salad (page 162)

Parantha with Ajwain, Fennel, and Chile Butter (page120)

Stuffed Okra (page 80)

3 GARAM MASALA

Chicken Pulao (page 152)

Classic Lamb Curry (page 100)

Crab Fried Rice (page 148)

Kidney Beans and Potato (page 78)

Lamb Kofta and Saffron Crème Fraîche (page 106)

Lamb Biryani (page 154)

Mussels in Chile, Ginger, and Curry Leaf Broth (page 96)

4 CUMIN SEEDS

Ayurvedic Detox Tea (page 220)

Kale, Chickpea, Mint, and Preserved Lemon Salad (page 162)

Khichadi (page 136)

Kidney Beans and Potato (page 78)

Lamb Biryani (page 154)

Lemon and Chickpea Rice (page 146)

South Indian Eggplant Pickle (page 184)

Tarka Dhal with Spinach and Fresh Tomato (page 60)

5 GROUND CUMIN

Bean and Lentil Salad with Garlic and Ginger (page168)

Classic Lamb Curry (page 100)

Lemon and Saffron Pot Roast Chicken (page 102)

Masala Roast Lamb (page 94)

Squid with Shallots, Ginger, and Chile (page 92)

Stuffed Okra (page 80)

6 CORIANDER SEEDS

Ayurvedic Detox Tea (page 220)

Basic Spiced Tomato Paste (page 237)

Cauliflower and Peas (page 68)

Lamb and Apricot Pasties (page 32)

Potato and Pea Samosas (page 50)

7
GROUND CORIANDER

Bean and Lentil Salad with Garlic and Ginger (page 168)

Chicken Korma (page 98)

Classic Lamb Curry (page 100)

Lamb Chops in Spiced Bread Crumbs (page 30)

Masala Roast Lamb (page 94)

Stuffed Potato and Pea Cakes (page 156)

8
MUSTARD SEEDS

Beet Curry (page 76)

Garlic, Ginger, and Chile Prawns (page 38)

Lemon and Chickpea Rice (page 146)

Mumbai Aloo (page 156)

South Indian Eggplant Pickle (page 184)

9
CASSIA OR CINNAMON STICKS

Ayurvedic Detox Tea (page 220)

Beef and Potato Curry (page 110)

Chana Masala (page 58)

Chicken Pulao (page 152)

Fish, Green Beans, and Spinach Kedgeree (page 22)

Lamb Biryani (page 154)

10
BAY LEAVES

Beef and Potato Curry (page 110)

Chicken Korma (page 98)

Chicken Pulao (page 152)

Lamb Biryani (page 154)

Lemon and Saffron Pot Roast Chicken (page 102)

11
GREEN CARDAMOM

Cardamom Coffee (page 218)

Chicken Korma (page 98)

Chicken Pulao (page 152)

Coconut Rice (page 138)

Lamb Biryani (page 154)

Masala Chai (page 212)

Orange and Carrot Balls with Chocolate (page 204)

12
SAFFRON

Lamb Biryani (page 154)

Lamb Kofta and Saffron Crème Fraîche (page 106)

Lemon and Saffron Pot Roast Chicken (page 102)

Pistachio Kulfi (page 200)

Saffron and Cashew Nut Rice (page 150)

13
COCONUT MILK POWDER

Salmon Baked with Crème Fraîche and Coconut (page 104)

Butter Chicken (page 114)

Creamy Peas and Mushrooms (page 64)

Fresh Tomato and Curry Leaf (page 88)

Spiced Coconut and Crème Fraîche Marinade (page 246)

14
CURRY LEAVES

Beet Curry (page 76)

Coconut Rice (page 138)

Fish in Tamarind Sauce (page 108)

Flaked Rice and Mixed Nut Poha (page 24)

Fresh Tomato and Curry Leaf (page 88)

Mussels in Chile, Ginger, and Curry Leaf Broth (page 96)

Shallots with Tamarind and Toasted Coconut (page 62)

15
TAMARIND PULP

Crab Fried Rice (page 148)

Fish in Tamarind Sauce (page 108)

Fresh Tomato, Date, and Tamarind Relish (page 176)

Shallots with Tamarind and Toasted Coconut (page 62)

Fruit Chutney (page 186)

Tamarind Rice (page 144)

light bites

CHAPTER 1

Fish, Green Beans, and Spinach Kedgeree

THIS IS A DELICIOUS AND RICH TAKE ON THE TRADITIONAL KEDGEREE RECIPE.
IF YOU DON'T EAT FISH, TRY THIS WITH A SPRINKLE OF SMOKED PAPRIKA
FOR A SMOKY EDGE AND ENJOY AS A VEGETARIAN OPTION.

SERVES 2 | PREPARATION TIME: 20 MINUTES | COOKING TIME: 15 MINUTES

FRESH

10 oz undyed smoked haddock

¼ leek or onion, finely chopped

2 garlic cloves, minced

4 oz green beans, trimmed and halved

4–5 teaspoons light cream

8 oz spinach, roughly chopped

Zest of 1 lemon

1 recipe cooked Simple Plain Rice
(page 134)

3 hard-boiled eggs,
peeled and quartered

SPICES

1-inch cassia or cinnamon stick

2 bay leaves

1 teaspoon fennel seeds

¼ teaspoon ground turmeric

¼ teaspoon red pepper flakes

PANTRY

1 tablespoon butter or oil

About ¼ cup vegetable or fish stock

Salt, to taste

1. Bring about 1¼ cups water to a boil in a large, shallow pan. Add the smoked haddock and simmer for 4 minutes, or until the fish is just cooked. Transfer to a plate and leave until cool enough to handle. Flake and set aside.

2. Heat the butter in a large frying pan over medium-low heat. Add the cassia, bay leaves, leek, garlic, and fennel seeds and fry until lightly browned. Reduce the heat slightly, add the turmeric, pepper flakes, and green beans and fry for 20 seconds.

3. Next, turn up the heat slightly and pour in the stock. Bring to a gentle simmer and cook for 4–5 minutes, or until the beans are al dente and the stock reduced. Stir in the cream and cook gently for 1–2 minutes, then gently stir in the spinach and salt. Turn off the heat; mix in the flaked haddock and lemon zest and combine with the cooked rice. Serve garnished with the boiled eggs.

Flaked Rice and Mixed Nut Poha

THIS DISH IS LIGHT YET FILLING AND IS A FAVORITE FOR BRUNCH
IN INDIA, TRADITIONALLY SERVED ALONGSIDE AN ARRAY OF
CHUTNEYS AND PICKLES. IT CAN ALSO BE EATEN ON ITS OWN OR AS AN
ACCOMPANIMENT TO GRILLED OR BROILED FISH OR MEAT.

SERVES 3–4 | PREPARATION TIME: 45 MINUTES | COOKING TIME: 15 MINUTES

FRESH

10–12 fresh curry leaves.

½ onion, finely chopped

2 medium potatoes, boiled with
skin on, cooled, and cubed

1 green chile, finely sliced (optional)

3 tablespoons finely chopped
cilantro

4 lemon wedges

SPICES

1 large pinch of asafetida

½ teaspoon mustard seeds

½ teaspoon whole cumin seeds

1 dried chile

¼ teaspoon ground turmeric

PANTRY

1 cup (5 oz) poha rice (dry flaked rice)

3 tablespoons oil

1 teaspoon salt, or to taste

½ teaspoon sugar

2 tablespoons roasted peanuts,
roughly chopped

1. Rinse the poha rice in a sieve gently but thoroughly under cold running water. Empty into a bowl, cover generously with fresh water, and leave to soak for about 5 minutes. Drain and leave in the sieve set over a bowl.

2. Heat the oil in a large nonstick frying pan over medium-high heat. After 2 minutes, add the asafetida, then reduce the heat slightly and keep stirring for 2 minutes. Add the mustard seeds, cumin seeds, and dried chile and fry for a further 1 minute.

3. Immediately toss in the curry leaves, turmeric, and salt. Add the onion and fry for 2–3 minutes, or until golden brown. Add the potatoes and sliced chile, if using, and continue to fry for a further 2 minutes, or until slightly brown.

4. Add the sugar, reduce the heat to low, and add the poha. Stir gently, while making sure everything is mixed together, and keep tossing thoroughly for 3–4 minutes. Turn off the heat, stir in the cilantro and peanuts, and squeeze the lemon wedges over. Serve hot or at room temperature.

Carrot and Chickpea Pancakes

THESE QUICK, WHEAT-FREE PANCAKES ARE PERFECT FOR ANY TIME
OF THE DAY AND CAN BE ENJOYED HOT OR COLD. STUFF THEM WITH
MUMBAI ALOO (PAGE 156) AND A DRIZZLE OF GARLIC AND
RED CHILE CHUTNEY (PAGE 178) TO MAKE A FILLING MEAL.

SERVES 2 | PREPARATION TIME: 30 MINUTES | COOKING TIME: ABOUT 4 MINUTES

FRESH

2-inch piece ginger, peeled
and finely chopped

2 green onions, finely chopped

1 carrot, grated

1 green chile, seeded
and finely chopped, or a large
pinch of red pepper flakes

1 tablespoon finely chopped cilantro

SPICES

¼ teaspoon ajwain seeds

¼ teaspoon ground cumin

PANTRY

1½ cups fine chickpea flour

½ teaspoon salt, or to taste

1–2 tablespoons ghee or oil

1. Place all the ingredients, except the ghee, into
a large bowl and mix, gradually adding 5–6 tablespoons
cold water, until the consistency of the batter resembles
that of heavy cream.

2. Dip some paper towels into the ghee or oil and carefully
wipe the inside of a nonstick crêpe or frying pan to coat the
entire pan. Heat the pan over medium heat, then gradually
pour in one ladleful of the batter and swirl the pan to get
a nice even layer.

3. Cook for 35–40 seconds, then gently lift up an edge
with a spatula to check if it is golden brown. Flip over
and cook the other side for 35–40 seconds. Continue this
process until all the batter is finished. Serve.

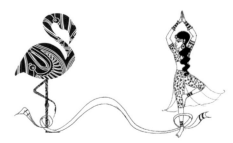

Vegetable Parantha Rolls

THESE HANDHELD WRAPS ARE GREAT PICNIC FOOD AND CAN BE A FUN WAY
TO INTRODUCE SPICES TO KIDS—JUST OMIT THE CHILES, IF YOU LIKE.
ADD SALAD LEAVES OR A SPOONFUL OF GREEN MANGO, APPLE, CILANTRO,
AND MINT RELISH (PAGE 174). PARANTHAS ARE EASY TO MAKE,
BUT FLATBREADS ARE JUST AS GOOD IF YOU ARE SHORT OF TIME.

SERVES 4 | PREPARATION TIME: 25 MINUTES | COOKING TIME: 5 MINUTES

FRESH

6 oz potatoes, peeled and
cut into cubes

8 oz carrots, cubed

1 scant cup (4 oz) peas

1-inch piece ginger, peeled
and finely shredded

1 green chile, finely chopped

1 tablespoon finely chopped cilantro

SPICES

1 teaspoon cumin seeds

2 teaspoons fenugreek leaves

½ teaspoon ground turmeric

1 teaspoon garam masala

PANTRY

2 tablespoons oil

Salt, to taste

1 teaspoon ghee, to drizzle

4 plain Paranthas (see Note page 120)
or flatbreads

1. Boil the potatoes and carrots for 4–5 minutes, or until almost tender. Add the peas and simmer for a few minutes more, then drain.

2. Heat the oil in a pan over medium-low heat. Add the cumin seeds and fry for 10 seconds. Next, add all the parboiled vegetables, ginger, green chile, fenugreek leaves, and salt and stir-fry for 30 seconds. Add the turmeric and garam masala and fry for a further 1 minute, then add the finely chopped cilantro. Turn the heat down to low, place a lid on top, and cook for a further 2–3 minutes, or until the vegetables are completely cooked through.

3. Take off the heat, drizzle with ghee, and slightly mash the vegetables with a fork. Let cool slightly and serve in the middle of a parantha or flatbread, either open or as a wrap.

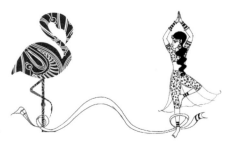

Lamb Chops in Spiced Bread Crumbs

RUSTIC AND LUXURIOUS ALL AT ONCE, THESE LAMB CHOPS MAKE A HEAVENLY CANAPÉ OR SPECIAL START TO A MEAL. TAKE CARE NOT TO OVERCOOK THE LAMB—IT SHOULD BE TENDER AND PINK WITHIN THE CRISP SPICED CRUMB.

SERVES 4 | PREPARATION TIME: 30 MINUTES
MARINATING TIME: 1–8 HOURS | COOKING TIME: 15 MINUTES

FRESH

10 lamb rib chops, French trimmed

2 garlic cloves, minced

½-inch piece ginger, peeled and finely grated

2 green chiles, finely chopped

2 cups fresh bread crumbs, made from stale bread

Zest of 1 lemon

2 tablespoons finely chopped cilantro

2 eggs

SPICES

2 teaspoons ground cumin

2 teaspoons ground coriander

2 teaspoons garam masala

PANTRY

2 tablespoons oil, plus extra for shallow-frying

½ teaspoon salt, or to taste

¼ cup all-purpose flour

1. Use your hands to flatten each chop, then place in a large bowl and massage in the garlic, ginger, chiles, ground cumin, and the 2 tablespoons oil. Cover with plastic wrap and chill for at least 1 hour, or preferably overnight.

2. Remove the lamb chops from the refrigerator and allow to come up to room temperature. Mix the bread crumbs with the lemon zest, cilantro, ground coriander, garam masala, and salt.

3. Next, whisk the eggs in a bowl, then spread the flour and spiced bread crumbs out on 2 separate plates.

4. Take 1 lamb chop at a time, coat in the flour, shaking off any excess, then dip in the egg, and finally, coat in the spiced bread crumbs. Place on a baking sheet and repeat with the remaining chops.

5. Heat enough oil in a large frying pan for shallow-frying over medium heat. Cook the chops, in batches, for 3 minutes on each side for medium-rare.

Lamb and Apricot Pasties

THESE LITTLE PASTIES ARE PACKED WITH DELICATE SWEET
AND SPICY FLAVORS. FOR AN AUTHENTIC RESULT, THE PASTRY
IS WELL WORTH ATTEMPTING, BUT TO CUT PREP TIME YOU CAN ALSO
USE FILO PASTRY FOR FRYING OR SHORTCRUST PASTRY FOR BAKING.

MAKES ABOUT 20 | PREPARATION TIME: 45 MINUTES | COOKING TIME: 1 HOUR

FRESH

1 lb freshly ground lamb

½ small onion, finely chopped

1 garlic clove, crushed

½-inch piece ginger, peeled and
grated or finely chopped

1 green chile, finely chopped

2 tablespoons finely chopped
cilantro or mint

1 recipe Rich Indian Pastry
(page 250)

SPICES

4 Whole Spice Bouquet Garni
(page 248)

1½ teaspoons cumin seeds

1½ teaspoons coriander seeds

1½ teaspoons garam masala

PANTRY

¼ cup dried apricots, finely diced

½–1 teaspoon salt, or to taste

2 tablespoons all-purpose flour

6 cups oil

1. In a heavy pan, combine the ground lamb, bouquet garni, cumin seeds, and coriander seeds.

2. Pour cold water into the pan to cover the lamb by ½ inch. Bring to a boil and boil over medium heat for about 40 minutes, stirring occasionally.

3. Add the onion, garlic, ginger, chile, apricots, garam masala, and salt. Reduce the heat to low and simmer, stirring occasionally, for a further 15 minutes, or until the liquid has evaporated. Let cool to room temperature, remove the bouquet garni, then stir in the cilantro.

4. Mix together the flour and 1 tablespoon water to make a sticky paste and set aside.

5. Divide the dough in half, roll out quite thinly, and, using a 4-inch cutter, cut out 9–10 circles. Repeat with the second half of the dough.

6. Place 1 tablespoon of filling in the middle of each circle, dip your finger into the sticky flour paste, and run your finger around the edges of the pastry circle.

7. Fold the pastry circle over to form a semicircle shape, then carefully pinch and seal all around the edges. Repeat until all the ingredients are used.

8. Heat the oil in a pan over medium heat. Fry the pasties 4 at a time for 3–4 minutes, or until the pastry is golden brown. Drain and serve hot or cold.

NOTE: Double-fry the pasties for a crispier pastry.

Fish Fritters

IF YOU LOVE BOTH FISH AND CHIPS AND SPICY FOOD, THIS RECIPE MAKES FOR A PERFECT COMBINATION. THE BATTER IS A LIGHTER ADAPTATION OF A CLASSIC PAKORA COATING AND IS MADE WITH SPARKLING WATER AND EGGS. SERVE WITH MAYONNAISE, A SQUEEZE OF LIME, AND A HANDFUL OF SHREDDED CILANTRO STIRRED THROUGH, OR SOME FRESH TOMATO, DATE, AND TAMARIND RELISH (PAGE 176).

SERVES 2–4 | PREPARATION TIME: 35 MINUTES
MARINATING TIME: 10–15 MINUTES | COOKING TIME: 25 MINUTES

FRESH
1 lb firm white fish such as haddock or cod, cut into medium strips
Juice of 1 lime
2 eggs

SPICES
¼ teaspoon chile powder
¼ teaspoon ajwain seeds
½ teaspoon ground cumin
½ teaspoon ground coriander
1 teaspoon tandoori masala

PANTRY
Salt, to taste
⅔ cup ice-cold sparkling water
1 cup all-purpose flour
½ cup cornstarch
Oil, for deep-frying

GARNISH
½ lime
1 green onion, cut into julienne
2 teaspoons chaat masala or sea salt (optional)

1. Place the fish pieces in a shallow dish and add salt, chile powder, and lime juice. Cover with plastic wrap and refrigerate for 10–15 minutes.

2. Whisk the eggs in a large, deep bowl, then pour in the sparkling water and mix quickly. Next, add the flour and cornstarch, ajwain seeds, ground cumin, ground coriander, tandoori masala, and salt. Stir gently with a fork, making sure not to overmix. The batter should have lumps.

3. Heat enough oil for deep-frying in a large pan or wok. Dip the fish pieces 3 at a time into the batter, then place straight into the hot oil and deep-fry, making sure you rotate them, for 3–5 minutes, or until the batter is golden brown. Remove with a slotted spoon and drain on paper towels. Repeat with the rest of the fish, then garnish with a squeeze of lime, green onion, and chaat masala, if you like.

NOTE: To test if the oil for deep-frying is hot enough, drop in a small piece of bread; if it browns in 20 seconds, it's ready.

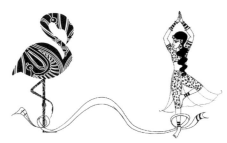

Cilantro and Chile Crab Balls

FRAGRANT SPICE AND DELICATE CRAB ARE SUCH AN IRRESISTIBLE COMBINATION,
YOU MIGHT WANT TO MAKE A DOUBLE QUANTITY OF THESE BITE-SIZE BALLS.

MAKES 15 | PREPARATION TIME: 50 MINUTES
COOKING TIME: 15 MINUTES

FRESH

10 oz white crabmeat

1 cup (8 oz) smooth mashed potatoes

5–6 green onions, finely chopped

1 garlic clove, minced

¼-inch piece ginger, peeled
and finely grated

2 red chiles, finely chopped

Zest of 1 lime, then ½ juiced

1 tablespoon finely chopped cilantro

1 egg, whisked

2 cups fresh bread crumbs

SPICES

1 teaspoon ground cumin

PANTRY

1 teaspoon salt, or to taste

3 tablespoons all-purpose flour

Oil, for deep-frying

OPTIONAL GARNISH

4-inch daikon, finely grated and
squeezed dry with a cloth

2 tablespoons finely chopped
cilantro

SERVE

1 lime, cut into wedges

1. In a large bowl, combine the crabmeat, mashed potatoes, green onions, garlic, ginger, chiles, lime zest, half the juice, the cilantro, ground cumin, and salt.

2. Using your hands, gently mix together and shape the mixture into round balls. Place each ball onto a lightly oiled plate and refrigerate for 15–20 minutes.

3. Meanwhile, put the egg into a bowl, then spread the flour and bread crumbs out on 2 separate plates. Heat enough oil in a deep pan or wok for deep-frying.

4. Take 1 crab ball at a time and lightly roll and coat first in the flour, then dip into the egg, and, finally, coat in the bread crumbs. Deep-fry in batches of 3–4 for 2–3 minutes, or until crisp and golden. Remove with a slotted spoon and drain on paper towels. Garnish with daikon and cilantro, if you like, and serve with lemon wedges.

NOTE: To test if the oil for deep-frying is hot enough, drop in a small piece of bread; if it browns in 20 seconds it's ready.

Garlic, Ginger, and Chile Prawns

THIS CLEVER DISH IS SO SIMPLE TO PREPARE AND COOK FOR A
RELAXED MEAL WITH FRIENDS. HAVE PLENTY OF CRUSTY BREAD
ON HAND TO DIP INTO AND SOAK UP ALL THE SPICED BUTTER.

SERVES 4 | PREPARATION TIME: 15 MINUTES | COOKING TIME: 5 MINUTES

FRESH

12 raw large prawns, peeled
with tails on

8 fresh curry leaves

4 garlic cloves, crushed

2-inch piece ginger, peeled and
sliced into thin sticks

1 large red chile, thinly sliced

SPICES

1 teaspoon black mustard seeds

PANTRY

1 cup ghee

½ tablespoon oil

Salt, to taste

GARNISH

2 tablespoons finely chopped cilantro

3 green onions, finely sliced

1. Preheat the oven to 400°F.

2. Heat the ghee in a medium pan over high heat and bring to a light boil.

3. Place 4 individual ramekin dishes on a baking sheet.

4. Carefully divide the hot ghee among the dishes and add 3 prawns to each dish.

5. Cook the prawns in the oven for 5 minutes, or until the prawns are cooked through.

6. Meanwhile, heat the oil in a small frying pan over medium-low heat. Add the mustard seeds and curry leaves and fry for 20 seconds, then add the garlic, ginger and red chile and fry for a further 20–30 seconds.

7. Divide the tempered spices among the prawn dishes, season with salt, and gently stir through.

8. Finish off by garnishing with cilantro and sliced green onions.

Sesame and Ginger Chicken Skewers

A SIMPLE, YET INDULGENT STARTER OR CANAPÉ, THESE SKEWERS ARE BEST SERVED WITH CILANTRO AND PEANUT CHUTNEY (PAGE 172). TO MAKE AHEAD, MARINATE THE CHICKEN THE NIGHT BEFORE, HOLDING OFF ON THE EGGS AND FLOUR UNTIL YOU ARE READY TO COOK.

SERVES 2–3 | PREPARATION TIME: 40 MINUTES
MARINATING TIME: 30 MINUTES–8 HOURS | COOKING TIME: 40 MINUTES

FRESH
2 chicken breasts
1 green chile, thinly sliced
1 garlic clove, crushed
3-inch piece ginger, peeled
2 tablespoons finely chopped cilantro
2 tablespoons fresh lime or lemon juice
1 egg white

SPICES
¾ teaspoon garam masala

PANTRY
⅓ cup white sesame seeds
2 tablespoons soy sauce
¼ teaspoon salt
Oil, for deep-frying
1 tablespoon all-purpose flour

OPTIONAL GARNISH
Honey, to drizzle

1. Cut each chicken breast into 8–9 pieces or cubes and place in a deep bowl.

2. Gently pulse the chile, garlic, ginger, cilantro, lime juice, garam masala, sesame seeds, soy sauce, and salt in a blender for 30–40 seconds.

3. Pour the mixture over the chicken pieces and, using your hands, gently rub into the pieces until coated. Cover and chill for 30 minutes, or overnight.

4. In a deep pan, heat the oil for deep-frying to 350°F.

5. Add the egg white and flour to the chicken and mix until everything is well coated. Deep-fry the chicken in 2 batches for 3–4 minutes on both sides until golden. Remove with a slotted spoon and drain on paper towels. Thread onto wooden skewers, lightly drizzle with honey, if you like, and serve immediately.

NOTE: To test if the oil for deep-frying is hot enough, drop in a small piece of bread; if it browns in 20 seconds it's ready.

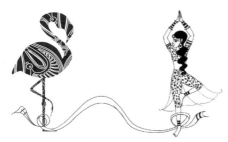

HOW TO MAKE
Paneer

PANEER IS AN INDIAN CHEESE WHERE THE MILK IS COAGULATED BY ADDING
A FOOD ACID. IT'S NOT A FERMENTED OR CURED PRODUCT LIKE OTHER CHEESES;
THE MILK CURDS ARE SIMPLY COLLECTED IN A CHEESECLOTH AND THEN HUNG
TO DRAIN OR PRESSED WITH A HEAVY WEIGHT. AFTER COOLING, A BLOCK OF FRESH
CHEESE HAS FORMED, WHICH CAN BE USED FOR MAKING A VARIETY OF DISHES.
ALTHOUGH PANEER IS AVAILABLE FOR PURCHASE, THERE IS SOMETHING
SPECIAL AND UNIQUE ABOUT MAKING YOUR OWN.

MAKES 2 CUPS (8 OZ) | PREPARATION TIME: 1–2 HOURS | COOKING TIME: 4–5 MINUTES

EQUIPMENT
HEAVY SAUCEPAN
THERMOMETER
COLANDER
CHEESECLOTH

heat

stir

strain

1
In a heavy saucepan, heat
1 quart whole milk. Bring the
milk to a temperature just
below the boiling point, then
turn off the heat. It should be
about 175°F.

2
Immediately add 3–4 tablespoons
of lemon juice, 1 teaspoon at a
time, gently stirring the milk after
each addition and making sure
the mixture doesn't stick to the
bottom of the pan. Keep stirring
until the milk separates and the
solid curds part from the green
and watery whey. Turn off the heat.

note You can always substitute lime
juice or white wine vinegar for
the lemon juice.

3
Let the curds and whey cool
for 30 minutes, or until still
warm, but at a temperature
you can handle. In the sink,
line a deep colander with a
large piece of cheesecloth.
Slowly strain the mixture
through the cheesecloth.
Rinse the curds gently with
fresh water.

4

Pull together the cheese-cloth corners, wrap around, and tie tightly into a knot. While doing so, squeeze out moisture from the curds. The more you squeeze, the firmer the resulting paneer will be.

note

This is tricky, so be gentle and patient.

5

In a sink, position the wrapped paneer in between 2 chopping boards. This way, you can force out more moisture and shape it into a firmer block, suitable for slicing and frying. To get a more rectangular shape, place something heavy like a pile of books, measuring weights, or a small pan of water straight on top of the chopping board. This will create extra pressure and give the cheese the familiar box shape. The longer you press the cheese, the firmer it gets—about 30–40 minutes is ideal.

squeeze

press

cut

6

Unwrap the paneer to find a firm block. Chop or slice the paneer into any shape or size you want. A great way to keep paneer soft is to soak the whole paneer block in a bowl of water and keep in the refrigerator. This way the paneer does not become hard. Alternatively, you can also soak the paneer in warm water after you have removed it from the refrigerator. Use it immediately, or refrigerate for up to 2 days. Paneer also freezes very well.

Paneer and Roasted Red Pepper Filo Cigars

PANEER IS A MELLOW CHEESE THAT CARRIES SPICE VERY WELL. YOU CAN MAKE THESE VEGETARIAN BITES WELL AHEAD: WRAP THE FILLING WITH THE FILO, BRUSH WITH BUTTER, AND THEN CHILL UNTIL READY TO BAKE. SWAP THE PEPPERS FOR BLANCHED SPINACH OR CHARBROILED EGGPLANTS, IF YOU LIKE.

MAKES 15 | PREPARATION TIME: 30 MINUTES | COOKING TIME: 15 MINUTES

FRESH

2 cups (8 oz) paneer (page 42)

⅓ package filo pastry

SPICES

3 teaspoons fenugreek leaves

1 teaspoon ground cumin

1 teaspoon ground coriander

1 teaspoon red pepper flakes

½ teaspoon dried mango powder

PANTRY

¼ cup (1 oz) jarred roasted red pepper, patted dry with paper towels

Salt, to taste

Flour, for dusting

½ cup melted ghee or butter, for brushing

OPTIONAL GARNISH

1 teaspoon each of ajwain seeds, fennel seeds, and onion seeds mixed together

1. Preheat the oven to 350°F and line a baking sheet with parchment paper.

2. Combine the paneer, roasted red pepper, fenugreek, ground cumin, ground coriander, pepper flakes, mango powder, and salt in a blender and gently pulse until well combined.

3. Lay a sheet of filo pastry on a floured work surface and brush with melted ghee, then lay another sheet on top and repeat. Cut the pastry into 3 strips.

4. Spoon the paneer and pepper filling along 1 edge of each of the pastry strips, leaving room to fold the pastry in at each end. Roll up into cigar shapes and lay, sealed edge down, on the prepared baking sheet. Repeat until all the filling is used.

5. Brush the cigars with ghee, sprinkle with the mixed seed garnish, if you like, and bake in the oven for about 15 minutes, or until golden brown.

NOTE: If using store-bought paneer, cut into cubes, drop into boiling water, and simmer for 5–7 minutes. Drain and then use.

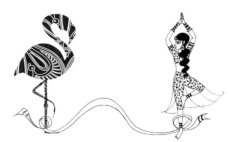

Chana Chaat / Bhel Puri

THIS STREET-STYLE SNACK IS A REAL TALKING POINT AND IDEAL
TO SERVE WITH DRINKS. IT'S ALL ABOUT THE CONTRASTS IN FLAVORS
AND TEXTURES, WITH SWEET, SOUR, CRUNCHY, AND SOFT ALL IN ONE BITE.

SERVES 4 | PREPARATION TIME: 20 MINUTES

FRESH

1 large potato, boiled with skin on,
cooled, and cut into small cubes

3 tablespoons Cilantro and
Peanut Chutney (page 172)

3 tablespoons Fresh Tomato, Date, and
Tamarind Relish (page 176)

⅓ cup pomegranate seeds,
1 tablespoon reserved

½ red onion, finely chopped

SPICES

½ teaspoon chaat masala

PANTRY

2 cups cooked chickpeas

8 tablespoons sev
(gram flour crispy noodles)

8 tablespoons puffed rice

2 tablespoons roasted cashews

1 teaspoon salt, or to taste

OPTIONAL GARNISH

Finely chopped cilantro, green onion,
mint, and red chile

1. In a large bowl, gently mix together the potato, chickpeas, sev, puffed rice, chutney, relish, pomegranate seeds, red onion, cashews, chaat masala, and salt. Taste and adjust the seasoning.

2. Garnish with reserved pomegranate seeds and, if you like, cilantro, green onion, mint, and red chile and serve immediately.

Chicken Tikka Wraps

HOMEMADE CHICKEN TIKKA, MARINATED AND BASTED WITH GHEE,
IS SUCCULENT AND SMOKY AND UTTERLY DELICIOUS WRAPPED AND
EATEN HOT IN FRESH NAAN BREAD (PAGE 127). THREAD BIG CHUNKS OF
PEPPER AND ONION ONTO THE SKEWERS TO MAKE THE FILLING MORE SUBSTANTIAL.
FOR AN EVEN MORE INTENSE CHARRED FLAVOR, COOK THE CHICKEN ON A GRILL.

SERVES 4 | PREPARATION TIME: 20 MINUTES
MARINATING TIME: 2–8 HOURS | COOKING TIME: 20 MINUTES

FRESH

14 oz skinless, boneless chicken thighs
1 recipe Tikka Masala Marinade
(page 246)
1 egg white
1 lime, cut into wedges
1 large tomato, thinly sliced
½ red onion, thinly sliced
Cucumber, Carrot, and Mint Chutney
(page 182)

SPICES

1 tablespoon chaat masala (optional)

PANTRY

1 tablespoon oil
2 tablespoons ghee, for basting
Naan (page 127)

1. Chop the chicken thighs into bite-size pieces. Place in a bowl and coat and mix well with the Tikka Masala Marinade. Cover with plastic wrap and leave to marinate in the refrigerator for 1–2 hours, or overnight.

2. Preheat the broiler. Either soak wooden skewers for 30 minutes before using or use metal ones. Add the egg white and oil to the chicken and mix until everything is well coated. Thread pieces of chicken 1 at a time onto each skewer. Line them up on a wire mesh rack on a baking sheet and cook under the broiler for 20 minutes, turning occasionally and basting with the ghee. Cook until the juices run clear.

3. Unthread each skewer onto a plate, sprinkle with the chaat masala, if you like, and a squeeze of lime.

4. Line up pieces of chicken in the middle of each bread, place slices of tomato and onion on top and drizzle with Cucumber, Carrot, and Mint Chutney. Fold in half, then slice the wrap in half.

NOTE: Only add the egg and oil to the chicken just before cooking.

VARIATIONS: Instead of chicken, use paneer, parboiled chunky mixed vegetables, or both. Shred the chicken, let cool, and stuff into pitas for lunchboxes.

Potato and Pea Samosas

MAKING SAMOSAS FROM SCRATCH IS AN EFFORT, BUT WORTHWHILE.
WHY NOT GET OTHERS TO JOIN IN, ROLLING, FILLING, AND
SEALING THE SAMOSAS ON YOUR OWN LITTLE PRODUCTION LINE?
IF YOU WOULD RATHER NOT FRY THE SAMOSAS, WRAP IN
STORE-BOUGHT PIE PASTRY AND BAKE INSTEAD.

MAKES 16 | PREPARATION TIME: 40 MINUTES | COOKING TIME: 30 MINUTES

FRESH
⅓ cup (2 oz) onion, finely chopped
⅓ cup (2 oz) cooked peas
2 small green chiles, thinly sliced
¼-inch piece ginger, peeled
1¼ lb potatoes, cooked, peeled, and
roughly mashed
3 tablespoons finely chopped cilantro
1 recipe Rich Indian Pastry
(page 250)

SPICES
1 tablespoon cumin seeds
1 tablespoon coriander seeds,
lightly crushed
½ teaspoon garam masala
½ tablespoon fenugreek leaves

PANTRY
2 tablespoons oil, plus extra
for deep-frying
1½ teaspoons salt, or to taste
1 tablespoon all-purpose flour,
plus extra for dusting

1. Heat the 2 tablespoons oil in a large frying pan over medium-low heat. Add the cumin seeds and coriander seeds and stir-fry for 20 seconds.

2. Add the onion, turn up the heat slightly, and fry for 3–4 minutes, or until the onion is golden brown. Add the cooked peas, garam masala, chiles, ginger, fenugreek, and salt and fry for 1 minute. Reduce the heat, mix in the mashed potato and chopped cilantro, and stir until well combined.

3. Mix together the flour and 2 tablespoons water to make a paste. Set aside.

4. In a deep pan, heat the oil for deep-frying to 350°F (see Note, page 52).

5. To assemble the samosas, divide the pastry dough in half, and divide each half into 4 small balls. Roll each ball into a circle about 5 inches wide. Cut each circle in half. Each half-moon will yield 1 samosa.

6. Add a spoonful of filling to the center of each half-moon. Dip your finger in the sticky flour paste and run along the edges. Fold the side in to form a cone, making sure to seal the edges tightly. Leave on a floured baking sheet. Work quickly to prevent the samosas from drying out. Shake off any excess flour and deep-fry until golden. Remove, drain on paper towels, and serve.

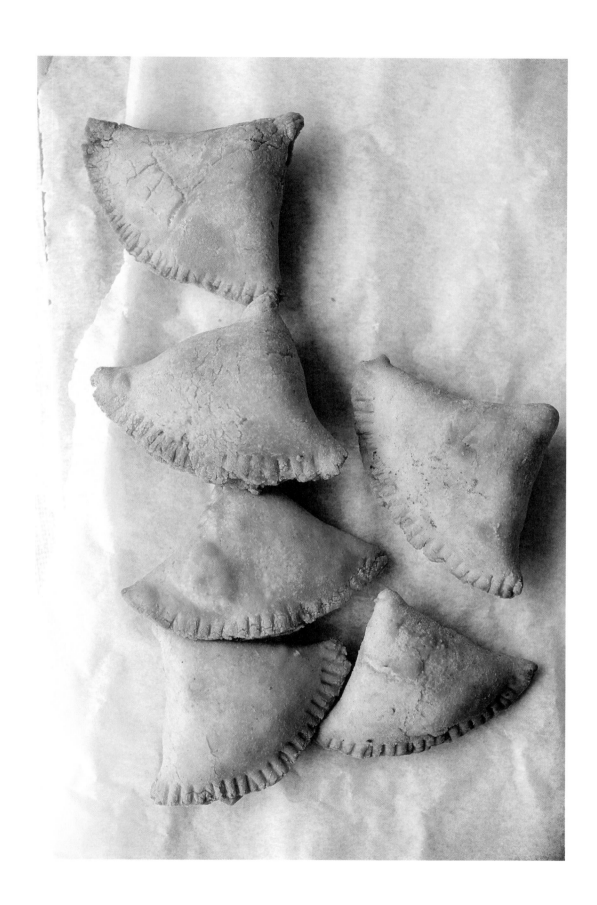

Alternative Samosa Fillings

ONCE YOU HAVE MASTERED THE BASIC RECIPE,
TRY ONE OF THESE DIFFERENT FILLING IDEAS.

NOTE:

To test if the oil for deep-frying is hot enough, drop in a small piece of bread; if it browns in 20 seconds, it's ready.

To prepare ahead, fry the samosas for 7–8 minutes, or until crisp but not yet golden, then put on a baking sheet and reheat in a preheated 400°F oven until crisp and hot through.

For very crispy, flaky samosas, fry them twice—once at 350°F and the second time around at 375°F. If you plan on freezing the samosas, fry them just once. Let cool completely and freeze in plastic freezer bags.

GROUND LAMB WITH PEAS AND MINT

Follow the recipe for Lamb and Apricot Pasties (page 32), omitting the apricots and replacing with cooked peas, and adding ½ teaspoon dried mint and ½ teaspoon chaat masala to the filling.

SHREDDED CARROT, CABBAGE, AND TOASTED PEANUTS

1. In a bowl, mix together 1⅓ cups (4 oz) shredded green cabbage, 2 grated carrots, ¼-inch piece ginger, peeled and grated, 1½ teaspoons toasted ground cumin, 2 tablespoons toasted finely crushed peanuts, 1 tablespoon finely chopped cilantro, and salt to taste.

2. Heat 1 tablespoon oil in a frying pan over medium-low heat, add 1 teaspoon black mustard seeds, 5–6 fresh curry leaves and 1 thinly sliced whole red chile and fry for 30–40 seconds, then add to the vegetables and mix together well.

SPINACH AND PANEER

1. Heat 1 tablespoon oil in a frying pan over medium-low heat. Add 2 teaspoons cumin seeds and fry for 20 seconds, then add a ¼-inch piece ginger, peeled and grated, 1 cup (4 oz) paneer, cut into tiny cubes, ½ tablespoon fenugreek leaves, 1 teaspoon garam masala, and salt to taste and fry for 1 minute over low heat.

2. Remove the pan from the heat and stir in 1 lb wilted and squeezed-dry spinach. Let cool completely.

SHREDDED DUCK, GREEN ONION, GINGER, AND CILANTRO

In a large bowl, mix together 1⅓ lb cooked shredded duck, 3 thinly sliced green onions, ½-inch piece ginger, peeled and grated, 2 teaspoons ground cumin, 1 tablespoon finely chopped cilantro, 4–5 finely chopped mint leaves, 1 minced large red chile, and salt to taste.

Lemon and Spice–Roasted Mixed Nuts

THINK OF THESE NOT JUST AS A SNACK TO ENJOY WITH DRINKS, BUT AS AN
INGREDIENT, TOO. TRY CRUSHED FOR TOPPING SALADS AND DIPS AND SCATTERING
OVER RICE DISHES. HAZELNUTS, PISTACHIOS, AND PECANS WOULD ALL WORK WELL,
PLUS YOU CAN REPLACE THE SUGAR WITH A HANDFUL OF RAISINS, IF YOU LIKE.

SERVES 4 | PREPARATION TIME: 10 MINUTES | COOKING TIME: ABOUT 30 MINUTES

FRESH

Zest and juice of 1 lemon

SPICES

1 teaspoon coarse black pepper

1 teaspoon ground cumin

1 teaspoon chile powder

½ teaspoon chaat masala

PANTRY

2 tablespoons melted coconut oil
or ghee or peanut oil

1 teaspoon light brown sugar

1 teaspoon sea salt, or to taste

1 cup cashews

1 cup walnuts

1 cup almonds

1 cup peanuts

1. Preheat the oven to 300°F.

2. In a large bowl, whisk together the oil, lemon zest and juice, all the spices, sugar, and salt. Next, add all the nuts and toss, making sure all the nuts are well coated.

3. Lay out the spiced nuts evenly on a baking sheet and toast in the oven for 20 minutes, making sure to toss and move the nuts around halfway through. Turn down the heat to 250°F and continue to bake for a further 10 minutes, or until golden brown.

4. Remove from the oven and let cool completely. Store in an airtight container for up to 8 days.

NOTE: Keep a close eye on the nuts during the last 5 minutes of roasting so that they don't burn.

vegetables and lentils

CHAPTER 2

Chana Masala

THIS RICH NORTH INDIAN CHICKPEA DISH IS TRADITIONALLY SERVED
WITH POORIS (PUFFED UP FRIED BREAD)—BUT ANY BREAD IS PERFECT.
ANY LEFTOVERS CAN BE DRIED OUT, DRIZZLED WITH FRESH TOMATO,
DATE, AND TAMARIND RELISH (PAGE 176), THEN SERVED WITH
FRIED PASTRIES OR STUFFED POTATO AND PEA CAKES (PAGE 156).

SERVES 4 | PREPARATION TIME: 30 MINUTES | COOKING TIME: 15 MINUTES

FRESH

1 large onion, roughly chopped

3 garlic cloves, roughly chopped

2-inch piece ginger, peeled
and roughly chopped

1½ green chiles, roughly chopped

2 tablespoons finely chopped cilantro
leaves, plus extra for garnish

4 teaspoons crème fraîche

SPICES

2 teaspoons fenugreek leaves

1 teaspoon panch phoran (page 13)

1 bay leaf

1-inch cassia or cinnamon stick

1 teaspoon ground turmeric

2 teaspoons garam masala

2 teaspoons ground cumin

PANTRY

3 tablespoons oil

2 x 15-oz cans chickpeas

2 tablespoons tomato purée

1 teaspoon salt, or to taste

OPTIONAL GARNISH

1 teaspoon ghee and
¼ teaspoon chaat masala

1. Heat 1 tablespoon of the oil in a pan and fry the onion, garlic, ginger, and green chiles for 6–7 minutes, or until soft and golden brown. Using a slotted spoon, transfer to a high-speed blender with 2 tablespoons of the chickpeas, the tomato purée, fenugreek leaves, and about ¾ cup water and blitz to a smooth paste.

2. Heat the remaining oil in the same pan over medium-low heat, add the panch phoran, bay leaf, and cassia cinnamon and fry for 30–40 seconds.

3. Pour in the chickpea paste and fry for 1 minute. Add the turmeric, garam masala, ground cumin, 1 tablespoon of the cilantro, and the salt and fry for a further 1 minute.

4. Mix in the remaining chickpeas and ¼ cup water, stir, then cover and simmer for 5–6 minutes. Stir in the crème fraîche and remaining cilantro and cook for a further 5 minutes, or until thick and creamy.

5. If using, drizzle with ghee and sprinkle with chaat masala. Garnish with cilantro or more ghee and chaat masala.

NOTE: Combining a small amount of cooked chickpeas with caramelized onions, garlic, and ginger helps create a thick, silky, and smooth base. This paste can be made a day in advance.

Tarka Dhal with Spinach and Fresh Tomato

A CLASSIC MIXED LENTIL DISH COOKED WITH WHOLE CUMIN SEED
AND GROUND SPICES, THEN GARNISHED WITH SMOKY BURNT GARLIC
AND CRISPY CURRY LEAVES, GINGER, AND CHILE. EASY AND QUICK
TO COOK, THIS IS PERFECT FOR FRIENDS OR FAMILY FOR SUPPER.

SERVES 4 | PREPARATION TIME: 20 MINUTES | COOKING TIME: 45 MINUTES

FRESH

¼ onion, finely chopped

2 garlic cloves, finely chopped

½-inch piece ginger, peeled
and finely chopped

3 large handfuls of baby
spinach, chopped

1 tomato, finely diced

SPICES

½ teaspoon ground turmeric

1 teaspoon cumin seeds

1 teaspoon garam masala

PANTRY

½ cup yellow moong dhal

⅓ cup masoor dhal

⅓ cup toor dhal

1 teaspoon salt, or to taste

3 tablespoons oil

Ghee, for drizzling

OPTIONAL GARNISH

Curry Leaves, Garlic, Ginger,
and Red Chile (page 240)

1. Combine all 3 dhals (lentils) and wash thoroughly. Put them into a large saucepan and cover with water. Bring to a boil over high heat, then reduce the heat to medium and simmer for 15 minutes. Using a large spoon, remove any white scum or residue.

2. Add the turmeric and salt and continue to simmer for a further 10 minutes, stirring occasionally and pressing the lentils against the pan with the back of your spoon. Cook until they are soft and creamy (add a little boiling water if too thick). Turn off the heat.

3. In a frying pan, heat the oil over medium-low heat. Add the cumin seeds and fry for 2–3 seconds. Turn up the heat slightly, add the onion and fry for 3–4 minutes, or until golden brown. Add the garlic and ginger and fry for 20 seconds.

4. Add the garam masala and fry for 1 minute, then pour in a ladleful of dhal, swirl around the pan, and pour it all back into the pan of cooked dhal. Simmer the dhal over low heat for 8–10 minutes.

5. Turn off the heat, add the chopped spinach and tomato, drizzle with ghee and garnish with the Curry Leaves, Garlic, Ginger, and Red Chile, if using.

Shallots with Tamarind and Toasted Coconut

THIS IS AN INTERESTING COMBINATION OF SWEET SHALLOTS, TOASTED COCONUT, AND SOUR TAMARIND, INFUSED WITH CHILES AND CRISPY CURRY LEAVES. THIS DISH WORKS WELL AS A SIDE DISH WITH DHALS AND MOST FLAVORED RICE AND INDIAN BREADS.

SERVES 2–3 | PREPARATION TIME: 15 MINUTES | COOKING TIME: 15 MINUTES

FRESH

5 oz shallots, peeled and halved
1 teaspoon Tamarind Pulp (page 228)
7–9 fresh curry leaves

SPICES

1 teaspoon crushed coriander seeds
1 teaspoon chile powder
¼ teaspoon ground turmeric
1 teaspoon mustard seeds
1 dried red chile

PANTRY

½ cup (1½ oz) desiccated coconut
3 tablespoons oil
½ teaspoon salt, or to taste

1. Heat a small frying pan over medium-low heat and toast the coconut and coriander seeds until golden brown. Add the chile powder, then turn off the heat and place in a high-speed blender. Blitz together, adding enough water, about 3–4 tablespoons, until it is a smooth paste.

2. Next, heat a pan over medium heat and pour in 2 tablespoons of the oil. Add the shallots and keep tossing and cooking until they are slightly browned. Add the salt, 3–4 tablespoons water, and the turmeric and cook for 5–7 minutes, or until soft. Add the coconut paste and tamarind pulp. Reduce the heat slightly and cook for 3–5 minutes.

3. Heat a large frying pan over medium-low heat. Pour in the remaining oil, add the mustard seeds and toss and fry for 20 seconds. Add the curry leaves and dried red chile and fry for 15 seconds. Finally, add the cooked shallots, gently toss everything together, then serve.

Creamy Peas and Mushrooms

A RICH AND SATISFYING DISH, THIS IS PRETTY QUICK TO MAKE AND DOESN'T
REQUIRE OR NEED ANY ONIONS OR CHILES. IT IS WONDERFUL AS PART OF ANY FAMILY
MEAL OR AS A SIMPLE BRUNCH DISH—JUST SERVE ON THICK SLICES OF TOASTED
BREAD. FRY THE MUSHROOMS AND PEAS WITH SPICES IN ADVANCE, THEN, WHEN
READY TO SERVE, STIR IN THE CREAM AND STOCK AND GENTLY SIMMER.

SERVES 4 AS A SIDE | PREPARATION TIME: 20 MINUTES | COOKING TIME: 15 MINUTES

FRESH

3 tablespoons light cream

8–9 fresh curry leaves

3 garlic cloves, minced

7–8 oz cremini mushrooms,
cut into quarters

1 cup (5 oz) cooked peas

½-inch piece ginger, peeled
and cut into julienne

SPICES

Large pinch of grated nutmeg

1 teaspoon black mustard seeds

1 teaspoon cracked black pepper

½ teaspoon garam masala

¼ teaspoon ground turmeric

¼ teaspoon paprika

PANTRY

1 tablespoon coconut milk powder

2 tablespoons oil

1 teaspoon salt, or to taste

6 tablespoons vegetable or chicken
stock or water

OPTIONAL GARNISH

Finely chopped cilantro, green onion,
and green or red chile

1. Mix together the light cream, coconut milk powder, and nutmeg and set aside for later.

2. Heat the oil in a heavy frying pan over medium-low heat. Add the mustard seeds and curry leaves and once they start to crackle and pop, add the garlic, and mushrooms. Turn up the heat slightly and fry, stirring frequently for 5 minutes, or until the mushrooms are a rich nutty brown.

3. Next, add the peas, pepper, garam masala, turmeric, paprika, and salt and cook, stirring, for 1 minute.

4. Now pour in the reserved cream paste and the stock. Turn down the heat and gently simmer for 4–5 minutes. Stir in the ginger and serve garnished with cilantro, green onion, and chile, if you like.

Baigan Bharta

To add a further intense smoky flavor, cook the eggplants over an open fire or barbecue. This can be done a day in advance. Any left over can be mixed with a little plain yogurt, finely chopped mint, and salt to taste and served at room temperature as a side dish.

SERVES 4 | PREPARATION TIME: 20–30 MINUTES | COOKING TIME: 30 MINUTES

FRESH

2 large Italian eggplants
3 medium onions, finely chopped
2–3 garlic cloves, finely chopped
½-inch piece ginger, peeled and finely shredded

SPICES

1 teaspoon panch phoran (optional)
½ teaspoon ground cumin
1 bay leaf
1-inch cassia or cinnamon stick
1 teaspoon fenugreek leaves
¼ teaspoon ground turmeric
1 teaspoon garam masala
½ teaspoon ground coriander

PANTRY

4 tablespoons oil
1 teaspoon salt, or to taste

OPTIONAL GARNISH

8 cherry tomatoes, halved or quartered and seeded if possible
1 tablespoon finely chopped cilantro

1. Preheat the broiler. Rub or brush ½ teaspoon of the oil all over the eggplants, then, using a fork, pierce a few random holes all over—this helps with the removal of the skin once cooled. Place under the broiler and cook, turning frequently, for about 15 minutes, or until the skin is charred black and smoky and the flesh buttery soft. Let cool, then gently peel and shred with a knife and fork and set aside.

2. Meanwhile, heat the remaining oil in a large, heavy frying pan over medium-low heat. Temper the following spices gently for 40 seconds: panch phoran, if using, followed by the cumin, bay leaf, and cassia.

3. Next, add the onions and fry gently for 4–5 minutes, or until soft and caramelized. Turn up the heat slightly, add the garlic and fenugreek leaves, and continue to fry for 1 minute. Stir in the turmeric, garam masala, ground coriander, ginger, and salt and fry for 1 minute, then add the cooked eggplant, mix well, and continue cooking, stirring frequently to avoid sticking, for 5–7 minutes. Cover and cook for a further 4 minutes. Serve garnished with tomatoes and cilantro, if you like.

Cauliflower and Peas

THERE ARE SEVERAL WAYS OF MAKING THIS DISH, BUT THIS ONE IS AN
EASYGOING AND SIMPLIFIED VERSION. CONSIDER OTHER VEGETABLES,
SUCH AS BUTTERNUT SQUASH OR BROCCOLI, OR EVEN PANEER. IF SHORT
ON TIME, PARBOIL THE CAULIFLOWER AND REDUCE THE COOKING TIME.

SERVES 4 | PREPARATION TIME: 15 MINUTES | COOKING TIME: 15 MINUTES

FRESH

2 lb cauliflower, cut into
bite-sized pieces

1 green chile, slit lengthwise
down the middle

1½ cups (8 oz) cooked peas

SPICES

1¼ teaspoons ground turmeric

2 teaspoons crushed coriander seeds

2 teaspoons crushed fennel seeds

1 teaspoon ground cumin

PANTRY

1 teaspoon all-purpose flour

½ teaspoon salt, or to taste

2 tablespoons mustard seed
or vegetable oil

6 tablespoons tomato purée

OPTIONAL GARNISH

Curry Leaves, Garlic, Ginger,
and Red Chile (page 240)

1. Place the cauliflower in a large bowl, sprinkle with the
flour, turmeric, salt, and 1 tablespoon of the oil and rub
into the florets until they are well coated.

2. Heat the remaining oil in a large frying pan or a wok over
medium heat. (If using mustard seed oil, see page 15.) Add
the cauliflower and green chile and keep tossing and frying
for 5–6 minutes, or until half-cooked and a little charred.

3. Add the coriander and fennel seeds and ground cumin
and fry for 1 minute.

4. Reduce the heat slightly, add the tomato purée and
cooked peas, then cover and continue to fry, stirring
frequently for 6–7 minutes, or until cooked through.

5. If you like, garnish with crispy curry leaves, garlic, ginger,
and red or green chile.

SIX
Eggs

1 MASALA SCRAMBLED EGGS

WHISK 8 eggs in a bowl, add 2 tablespoons cream or milk, and whisk together.

HEAT 1 tablespoon oil in a heavy frying pan over low heat.

ADD ½ teaspoon cumin seeds and 1-inch piece ginger and fry gently for 10 seconds.

ADD ½–1 teaspoon garam masala, 1 teaspoon red pepper flakes, and a little salt and fry for 1 minute.

POUR in the eggs and reduce the heat. Stir gently from side to side until almost a creamy consistency.

DRIZZLE with 2 teaspoons ghee and sprinkle with finely chopped cilantro.

SERVE with plain paranthas (see Note, page 120) or toasted English muffins.

2 SPICED EGGY BREAD

WHISK 6 eggs in a large wide, flat bowl.

ADD 1 teaspoon garam masala, 1 teaspoon red pepper flakes, ½ teaspoon ground cumin, ½ teaspoon ground coriander, 1 tablespoon fenugreek leaves, 2 tablespoons finely chopped cilantro, and ½ teaspoon salt. Whisk everything together.

PLACE a heavy frying pan over medium heat.

ADD 2 tablespoons oil and a large knob of butter. Take 4–5 thin slices of bread, dip 1 slice of bread at a time into the egg mixture, pressing gently.

FLIP over until well coated. Leave to soak for a minute or two.

PLACE your bread slices into the hot pan and fry until golden and crisp on both sides.

SERVE immediately.

3 COCONUT EGG CURRY

HEAT the oil in a wok or heavy pan and gently fry 6 peeled soft-boiled eggs for 1 minute, or until lightly golden. Remove and reserve.

ADD 1 tablespoon Ginger and Garlic Paste (page 231), 1 tablespoon Caramelized Onion Paste (page 231), followed by 1½ teaspoons ground turmeric, 1½ teaspoons garam masala, 1 teaspoon ground cumin, and ½ teaspoon salt.

FRY for 30–35 seconds while gently tossing, then stir in ⅔ cup coconut milk and simmer gently over medium heat for 2–3 minutes.

ADD 2 sliced green chiles and 2½-inch peeled and shredded ginger and simmer for 5 minutes, or until the sauce has thickened. Halve the eggs and add to the sauce, yolk side up. Sprinkle with finely chopped green onion and cilantro.

SERVE with Lemon and Chickpea Rice (page 146).

4 NARGISI EGG KOFTA

BLEND 1 finely chopped small onion (squeezed dry in a cloth), 5 finely chopped garlic cloves, 1 tablespoon chopped ginger, ½ teaspoon garam masala, ½ teaspoon ground cumin, ½ teaspoon ground coriander, a pinch of nutmeg, 1 teaspoon salt, ½ teaspoon chopped mint, and 1 tablespoon chopped cilantro.

BLITZ until finely chopped, then add 1 lb ground lamb and blitz again until it is a smooth paste.

DIVIDE the paste into 4 portions. Flatten and shape around 4 peeled soft-boiled eggs.

ROLL each kofta in ¼ cup all-purpose flour, then 1 beaten egg, and last, fresh bread crumbs (3 slices of bread, crusts off). Chill for 30 minutes.

HEAT 6 cups oil over medium-high heat and fry 2 koftas at a time for 8–10 minutes. Cut in half.

SERVE with Fresh Tomato, Date, and Tamarind Relish (page 176).

5 ROASTED VEGETABLES AND BAKED EGGS

PREHEAT the oven to 375°F.

COAT 8 oz cubed eggplant, 1 cubed yellow pepper, and 1 chopped red onion with 2 tablespoons oil, 1 teaspoon salt, 1 teaspoon crushed fennel seeds, and ½ teaspoon red pepper flakes.

PLACE on a heavy baking sheet and roast for 15–20 minutes, tossing frequently.

TOSS with the Tomato and Mustard Dressing (page 74) and pour into a shallow ovenproof dish.

MAKE 4–5 evenly spaced wells and crack 1 egg into each well. Season with salt and pepper and bake for 10–12 minutes.

GARNISH with finely chopped cilantro and a pinch of toasted crushed cumin seeds.

SERVE with warm crusty bread.

6 SPINACH AND POTATO OMELETTE

HEAT 2 tablespoons oil in a large nonstick ovenproof frying pan.

TOSS in 2 teaspoons whole cumin seeds, then stir in 1 lb cooked cubed potatoes and 3 finely sliced green onions and fry for 2 minutes.

WHISK 6 eggs in a large bowl and season with ½ teaspoon salt and ½ teaspoon pepper. Mix in 8 oz cooked chopped spinach, 1 teaspoon fenugreek leaves, and ½ teaspoon red pepper flakes.

POUR the egg mixture into the frying pan. Cover and cook, without stirring, for about 6 minutes, or until cooked but soft on top.

FINISH cooking under a hot broiler until golden brown. Cut into quarters.

SERVE with Shredded Raw Veg Salad (page 160).

Dhal Makhani

Make this mixed lentil and bean combination on special occasions, as it is the ultimate dhal dish. Traditionally, it takes hours to cook, but good-quality cooked legumes work just as well. The smoky garlic mixed with the fenugreek leaves and chile and combined with cream and butter certainly make this dish heavenly, lavish, and indulgent.

SERVES 4 | PREPARATION TIME: 30 MINUTES | COOKING TIME: 25–30 MINUTES

FRESH

1 large onion, roughly chopped

4 garlic cloves, roughly chopped

1-inch piece ginger, peeled and roughly chopped

1 small green chile, roughly chopped

2 tablespoons finely chopped cilantro

SPICES

1½ teaspoons fenugreek leaves

1 teaspoon cumin seeds

1-inch cassia or cinnamon stick

1 bay leaf

1 black cardamom pod, slightly crushed

1½ teaspoons garam masala

¼ teaspoon ground turmeric

PANTRY

3 tablespoons ghee or oil

½ cup cooked whole black urad dhal, reserving ½ tablespoon

½ cup cooked kidney beans, reserving ½ tablespoon

2 teaspoons tomato purée

1 teaspoon salt, or to taste

GARNISH

1 teaspoon melted ghee

½ tablespoon heavy cream

1 tablespoon finely chopped cilantro

1. Heat 1 tablespoon of the ghee in a large frying pan over medium-low heat and fry the onion, garlic, ginger, and green chile for 7–8 minutes, or until soft and golden brown. Let cool slightly, then transfer with a slotted spoon to a high-speed blender together with the reserved ½ tablespoon urad dhal and ½ tablespoon kidney beans, the tomato purée, fenugreek leaves, and ¼ cup water and blitz to a smooth paste.

2. Heat the remaining oil in a frying pan over medium-low heat. Add the cumin seeds, cassia, bay leaf, and black cardamom and fry for 20 seconds. Add the onion and bean paste and stir-fry for 2 minutes.

3. Add the garam masala, turmeric, and salt and fry for 1 minute.

4. Next, add the urad dhal, kidney beans, cilantro, and up to ½ cup water, then cover and continue simmering for 10 minutes, or until thick and creamy.

5. Turn off the heat and garnish with the ghee, cream, and chopped cilantro.

NOTE: Combining a small amount of cooked legumes and beans with the caramelized onions, garlic, and ginger helps to create a thick, silky, and smooth base. This paste can be made a day in advance.

Steamed Green Beans in Tomato and Mustard Dressing

THESE BEANS COMPLEMENT MOST ROASTS OR GRILLED MEATS, SALADS, AND SAVORY TARTS. THIS SIDE DISH HAS A DELICIOUS DRESSING, WHICH CAN ALSO BE USED WITH COOKED POTATOES, PEAS, FAVA BEANS, OR LONG-STEMMED BROCCOLI. PREPARE THE DRESSING 1–2 DAYS IN ADVANCE, THEN WHEN DRESSING THE SALAD MAKE SURE THE BEANS ARE HOT—THAT WAY THEY WILL ABSORB ALL THE FLAVORS.

SERVES 4 | PREPARATION TIME: 15 MINUTES | COOKING TIME: 15 MINUTES

FRESH
8 oz green beans, trimmed
6–7 fresh curry leaves
1 garlic clove, minced

SPICES
¼ teaspoon black mustard seeds
¼ teaspoon chile powder
¼ teaspoon ground coriander
¼ teaspoon ground black pepper
¼ teaspoon ground turmeric
¼ teaspoon ground cinnamon

PANTRY
2 tablespoons mustard seed oil or vegetable oil
¾ cup (6 oz) tomato purée
Large pinch of sugar
Salt, to taste

GARNISH
Crispy Ginger, Onion, and Garlic (page 238)

1. Steam the green beans for 4–5 minutes, then drain and plunge into ice-cold water.

2. Pour the oil into a heavy pan and heat over medium heat for 1 minute. (If using mustard seed oil, see page 15.) Add the curry leaves and black mustard seeds and fry for 30 seconds. Turn down the heat, add the garlic and fry for 2 seconds, then add the chile powder, ground coriander, black pepper, turmeric, ground cinnamon, and sugar and fry for a further 1 minute.

3. Stir in the tomato purée and salt and cover. Turn up the heat slightly and cook for a further 5–8 minutes, stirring occasionally, until the oil starts to separate from the tomato dressing.

4. Pour the dressing over the green beans, garnish with the Crispy Ginger, Onion, and Garlic, and serve hot or cold.

Beet Curry

Delicious hot or cold, beet curry is a fantastic main course or accompaniment. Whether you are a vegetarian or not, this colorful, mouthwatering dish is a healthy option that can be enjoyed with a salad or with rice and chapati. Remember to ensure that the beet chunks are roughly equal in size.

SERVES 4 | PREPARATION TIME: 30 MINUTES | COOKING TIME: 40 MINUTES

FRESH

2 green chiles, slit lengthwise down the middle

1-inch piece ginger, peeled and roughly chopped

14–16 oz red beets

10 fresh curry leaves

1 onion, finely chopped

SPICES

Seeds from 4 black cardamom pods

½ teaspoon fennel seeds

2 teaspoons black mustard seeds

1 teaspoon ground cumin

1 teaspoon ground turmeric

½ teaspoon chile powder

PANTRY

⅓ cup (1 oz) desiccated coconut

3 tablespoons vegetable oil

1 teaspoon salt, or to taste

SERVE

1 cup plain yogurt

1. In a mixer or grinder, place the coconut, chiles, ginger, black cardamom seeds, and fennel seeds and grind firmly, adding a little water if necessary. Set aside.

2. Cut the beets into same-sized wedges or cubes and cook in a saucepan of boiling water for 20 minutes, or until tender, then drain and set aside.

3. Heat the oil in a large frying pan. Add the mustard seeds and as they begin to pop, add the curry leaves. Immediately stir in the beets, onion, cumin, turmeric, chile powder, and salt and cook for 7–8 minutes, stirring frequently. Stir in the coconut spice mix, then reduce the heat and cook for a further 5 minutes over medium heat, stirring frequently and gradually adding water to loosen, then cook for a further 5–7 minutes.

4. Remove the pan from the heat and serve with the yogurt on top.

Kidney Beans and Potato

THE ULTIMATE IN COMFORT FOOD, AND A WARMING WINTER DISH,
THIS RUSTIC STEW HAS A DENSE MASALA-BASED SAUCE, WHICH
IS BEST SERVED AND SOAKED UP WITH SIMPLE PLAIN RICE (PAGE 134).

SERVES 4 | PREPARATION TIME: 20 MINUTES | COOKING TIME: 25 MINUTES

FRESH

2 onions, roughly chopped

4 garlic cloves, roughly chopped

1-inch piece ginger, peeled
and roughly chopped

1½ green chiles, roughly chopped

1 potato, cubed into 8 pieces

2 tablespoons finely chopped cilantro,
plus extra for garnish

SPICES

2 teaspoons fenugreek leaves

1½ teaspoons cumin seeds

2 teaspoons garam masala

1 teaspoon ground turmeric

1 teaspoon ground coriander

PANTRY

3 tablespoons oil

4 cups (28 oz) cooked kidney beans,
reserving 2 tablespoons

1 tablespoon tomato purée

Hot water, as needed

1 teaspoon salt, or to taste

1 tablespoon melted ghee

1. Heat 1 tablespoon of the oil in a pan and fry the onions, garlic, ginger, and green chiles for 6–7 minutes, or until soft and golden brown. Let cool slightly, then, using a slotted spoon, transfer to a blender together with the 2 tablespoons reserved kidney beans, the tomato purée, fenugreek leaves, and 2 tablespoons hot water and blitz to a smooth paste.

2. Heat the remaining oil in a frying pan over medium-low heat, add the cumin seeds, and fry for 2–3 seconds. Add the onion and bean paste and fry for 2 minutes. Add the garam masala, turmeric, ground coriander, and salt and fry for 1 minute, then add the potato and about ½ cup hot water. Cover and simmer for 5 minutes. Next, add the kidney beans and cilantro and continue simmering for 4–5 minutes, or until the sauce is thick and creamy and the potato is cooked through.

3. Drizzle with the ghee and garnish with cilantro.

NOTE: Combining a small amount of cooked kidney beans with caramelized onions, garlic, and ginger helps to create a thick, silky, and smooth base. This paste can be made a day in advance.

Stuffed Okra

It's the crisp and fresh texture that makes okra the perfect vegetable for this dish. Once you get rid of okra's natural sliminess by trimming the tops and adding lemon juice, the incredible flavors of the stuffing ooze out and complement the mild taste of this "lady's finger" (as okra is sometimes referred to in India). Stuffed okra is equally good as a side dish or a main course. Make sure they are super-dry before preparing.

SERVES 4 | PREPARATION TIME: 45 MINUTES | COOKING TIME: 20 MINUTES

FRESH

1 lb okra

1 red onion, finely sliced

1 red pepper, cut into strips

1-inch piece ginger, peeled and finely sliced

2 teaspoons lemon juice

SPICES

2 teaspoons ground coriander

2 teaspoons ground cumin

1 teaspoon red pepper flakes

1 teaspoon ground turmeric

½ teaspoon pomegranate seed powder (optional)

PANTRY

1 tablespoon desiccated coconut

Salt to taste

2–3 tablespoons oil

1. Wash and then wipe the okra until absolutely dry. Carefully remove the stalks (making sure not to cut too far down), then slit each down the middle from top to tail without cutting all the way through.

2. Mix the ground coriander, ground cumin, red pepper flakes, turmeric, pomegranate seed powder, if using, desiccated coconut, the lemon juice, and ¼ teaspoon salt, into a paste. Using a small teaspoon, stuff each okra with this masala paste, pushing it in gently with your finger. Reserve the leftover masala.

3. Heat the oil in a wok or large frying pan over medium heat. Add the sliced onion and cook for 30 seconds, then add the stuffed okra and fry for 5 minutes, tossing gently.

4. Cover and cook over low heat, stirring occasionally. Add the red pepper, sliced ginger, and salt, turn up the heat to medium, and stir-fry gently for 5–7 minutes. Cover again and cook for a further 5–6 minutes.

5. Stir in the reserved masala paste when the okra is almost cooked. Cover and cook over low heat for 1–2 minutes, or until the okra is fully tender and darker in color.

Wilted Spinach with Ginger, Garlic, and Almonds

THIS IS A HUMBLE YET SURPRISING DISH THAT CAN BE MADE IN MINUTES. CHOOSE GOOD-QUALITY FRESH SPINACH OR EVEN CONSIDER USING SHREDDED KALE. THE LAVISH GARNISH TAKES THIS DISH TO ANOTHER LEVEL.

SERVES 4 AS A SIDE | PREPARATION TIME: 20 MINUTES | COOKING TIME: 3 MINUTES

FRESH

1 tablespoon finely chopped onion

1 large red chile, finely sliced

1¼ lb fresh spinach, wilted or cooked, squeezed dry of all water, and roughly chopped

2 tablespoons light cream

SPICES

¼ teaspoon ground turmeric

¼ teaspoon ground cumin

PANTRY

1 tablespoon oil

Salt, to taste

GARNISH

Crispy Ginger, Onion, and Garlic (page 238)

1 tablespoon lightly toasted sliced almonds

1 teaspoon melted ghee

1. Heat the oil in a frying pan, then add the onion and fry for 2 minutes, or until golden brown.

2. Reduce the heat, add the turmeric and fry for about 30 seconds. Stir in the red chile, cumin, and salt, then stir in the spinach and cream and gently cook over low heat for 30 seconds.

3. Garnish with the Crispy Ginger, Onion, and Garlic, toasted almonds, and a drizzle of ghee.

Charred Broccoli with Chile and Fennel

YOU MAY THINK THAT THIS DISH IS RELAXED, BUT DON'T BE DECEIVED—THE CHARRED BROCCOLI AND INTENSE COMBINATION OF FENNEL, CRISPY GINGER, AND GARLIC MAKE AN IMPRESSIVE STATEMENT. OTHER VEGETABLES TO CONSIDER USING ARE ZUCCHINI WEDGES, SLICED SWEET POTATOES, OR EGGPLANT BATONS.

SERVES 4 | PREPARATION TIME: 10 MINUTES | COOKING TIME: 6 MINUTES

FRESH
2 garlic cloves, finely sliced

1 large red chile, seeded if you like and finely sliced

1⅓ lb broccoli spears, halved lengthwise

1-inch piece ginger, peeled and cut into julienne

SPICES
2 teaspoons fennel seeds

1 teaspoon mustard seeds

PANTRY
1½ tablespoons oil

Salt, to taste

GARNISH
Toasted Coconut, Pomegranate Seeds, and Cilantro (page 238)

Handful of cilantro leaves and stalks

1. Heat the oil in a large deep frying pan over medium-low heat. Add the fennel seeds and mustard seeds and fry until they crackle and pop.

2. Add the garlic, chile, and broccoli and fry until the broccoli is slightly charred in color. Reduce the heat, cover, and cook for 4–5 minutes, or until cooked through.

3. Uncover, season with salt, and add the ginger. Toss and gently cook for 20 seconds.

4. Garnish with a scattering of Toasted Coconut, Pomegranate Seeds, and Cilantro and additional cilantro leaves and stalks.

NOTE: You can also blanch the broccoli spears for 1–2 minutes in boiling salted water, then drain.

Eggplant with Chile and Pomegranate Dressing

THIS IS AN UPDATED VERSION OF "TAWA BAINGAN." COOK THE EGGPLANT SLICES
UNTIL CRISP AND GOLDEN, THEN COAT AND LEAVE TO INFUSE IN THE SWEET CHILE
DRESSING. ENJOY AS A WARM SALAD OR SIDE DISH SERVED ALONGSIDE ANY
HOT CURRIES, FRIED PASTRIES, AND SPICED MEATS OR BAKED FISH.
ALTERNATIVELY, THE DRESSING CAN BE SERVED ON THE SIDE.

SERVES 2 AS A MAIN OR 4 AS A SIDE | PREPARATION TIME: 1 HOUR
COOKING TIME: 45 MINUTES

FRESH

2–3 small-medium Italian eggplants,
or medium ones sliced lengthwise,
small ones cut in half and scored

2 shallots, finely chopped

1 garlic clove, minced

1 tablespoon finely chopped cilantro

1 tablespoon finely chopped mint

2–3 tablespoons pomegranate seeds

SPICES

1 tablespoon garam masala

¼ teaspoon ground turmeric

1 teaspoon red pepper flakes

PANTRY

3–4 teaspoons salt, or to taste

2 tablespoons oil, plus extra for brushing

1 tablespoon sugar

3 tablespoons sherry wine vinegar

1. Sprinkle the eggplant slices with salt, place in a colander set over a bowl, and leave to stand for 30 minutes. Rinse the eggplant and pat dry.

2. Combine the garam masala and turmeric in a small bowl, add the oil, and stir together to make a paste. Set aside.

3. In a small saucepan over medium heat, combine the shallots, garlic, sugar, vinegar, red pepper flakes, and 3 tablespoons water. Bring to a boil and cook for 1 minute, then remove from the heat and let cool completely. Stir in the cilantro, mint, and pomegranate seeds.

4. Rub both sides of the eggplant slices with the mixed spice paste.

5. Heat a griddle pan to high and brush the grates or bars with vegetable oil, then cook the eggplant until charred and tender, turning over halfway through, about 8–9 minutes.

6. Arrange the eggplant slices on a platter and spoon the dressing mixture over the top.

NOTE: Salting the eggplant removes some of its water, which makes for better searing.

Fresh Tomato and Curry Leaf

ALTHOUGH THIS IS A SIMPLE TOMATO DISH, IT MAKES A PERFECT
SIDE-DISH PARTNER FOR MOST MAIN MEAT, VEGETABLE, AND RICE DISHES.
HOWEVER, IT CAN ALSO BE A STAND-ALONE DISH. ENJOY WITH
HOT BUTTERED NAAN (PAGE 127) OR TOASTED CRUSTY BREAD.

SERVES 2–4 | PREPARATION TIME: 15 MINUTES | COOKING TIME: 15 MINUTES

FRESH

8 tomatoes, peeled,
quartered, and seeded

1 onion, finely chopped

3 garlic cloves, roughly chopped

8–9 fresh curry leaves

SPICES

5 whole dried chiles, soaked in
¼ cup hot water for 5 minutes

¼ teaspoon ground turmeric

1½ teaspoons garam masala

1 teaspoon ground cinnamon

Large pinch of nutmeg

1 teaspoon mustard seeds

PANTRY

2 tablespoons tomato purée

¼ teaspoon sugar

2 teaspoons coconut milk
powder (optional)

Hot water, as needed

2 tablespoons mustard seed oil or
vegetable oil

Salt, to taste

OPTIONAL GARNISH

Crispy Okra (page 232)

Fresh cilantro leaves

1. Combine the following in a blender and blitz to form
a fine, smooth paste: 1 tomato quarter, the onion, garlic,
soaked chiles (including the soaking water), tomato purée,
turmeric, sugar, garam masala, ground cinnamon, nutmeg,
coconut milk powder, if using, and 1 tablespoon hot water.

2. Heat the oil in a large frying pan over medium-low heat.
(If using mustard seed oil, see page 15.) Add the mustard
seeds and curry leaves and fry for 20 seconds.

3. Turn down the heat and stir in the onion paste and salt.
Keep stirring and frying
for 1–2 minutes.

4. Add about 2 tablespoons hot water, cover, and simmer
gently for 10 minutes, then add the remaining tomatoes,
stir through and cook for 1 minute. Turn off the heat and
garnish with Crispy Okra and cilantro, if you like.

fish, meat, and poultry

CHAPTER 3

Squid with Shallots, Ginger, and Chile

A SEAFOOD-LOVER'S ESSENTIAL, THIS SPICED SQUID BURSTS WITH THE
SUBTLE YET UNMISTAKABLE TASTE OF THE INDIAN TRINITY OF SHALLOTS,
GINGER, AND RED CHILE—TRANSPORTING YOU TO THE BEACHES OF KERALA,
WHERE INDIAN CIVILIZATION BEGAN. SERVE THIS IMPRESSIVE DISH
AS A STARTER, LIGHT LUNCH, OR DINNER PARTY COURSE.

SERVES 4 | PREPARATION TIME: 20 MINUTES | COOKING TIME: 15 MINUTES

FRESH

2 lb fresh squid, dried well, scored and
cut into thick strips, tentacles included

8–10 fresh curry leaves

3 shallots or 1 onion, finely sliced

4-inch piece ginger, peeled
and finely shredded

1 large red chile, seeded if you like and
finely sliced

2 tomatoes, finely chopped

Juice of ½ lime or lemon

1 tablespoon finely chopped cilantro

SPICES

1 teaspoon chile powder

1 teaspoon ground cumin

1 teaspoon ground coriander

½ teaspoon ground turmeric

PANTRY

Large pinch of cracked black pepper

½ cup all-purpose flour or
6 tablespoons cornstarch

½ teaspoon salt, or to taste

⅔ cup oil

1. In a large bowl, combine the flour, salt, black pepper, chile powder, ground cumin, ground coriander, and turmeric. Mix well and add the squid pieces. Using clean, dry hands, toss the squid gently in the flour mix, making sure each piece is evenly coated.

2. Heat 3 tablespoons of the oil in a large frying pan or wok over medium-low heat. Add the curry leaves, followed by the shallots, and fry for 2–3 minutes. Turn the heat up to medium, add the ginger and red chile and stir-fry until crisp and golden brown. Remove from the pan with a slotted spoon and drain on paper towels.

3. Using the same pan or wok, heat the remaining oil over medium-low heat. Add the squid in 2 batches and fry for 3–5 minutes, or until crisp and cooked through. Remove the squid with a slotted spoon to drain.

4. Mix the squid together with the crispy shallot mix. Add the tomatoes and toss together gently. Finish off with a squeeze of lime and the cilantro.

NOTE: Be careful not to overcook the squid.

Masala Roast Lamb

Cooking meat on the bone definitely creates more flavor, as proved by this classic recipe, which is a perfect twist to a traditional family roast dinner. Enjoy this dish with buttered steamed vegetables and green salad, or finely sliced and wrapped inside Naan bread (page 127).

SERVES 4–6 | PREPARATION TIME: 1½ HOURS
MARINATING TIME: 2–8 HOURS | COOKING TIME: 4 HOURS

FRESH
4–5 lb leg of lamb or shoulder

1 lb onions, chopped

3–4 green chiles

10 garlic cloves, finely chopped

1½-inch piece ginger, peeled and finely grated

2 cups (16 oz) Greek yogurt, lightly whisked

SPICES
2 tablespoons ground cumin

3 tablespoons ground coriander

1 teaspoon garam masala

4 bay leaves

Two 1-inch cassia or cinnamon sticks

13 green cardamom pods, slightly cracked

12 black peppercorns

8 cloves

PANTRY
½ cup ground almonds

2 teaspoons salt, or to taste

4 tablespoons oil

OPTIONAL GARNISH
1 lemon, cut into wedges

1. Using a sharp knife, make deep slits all over the lamb, then place it in the center of a well-greased sheet pan.

2. Blitz the onions, almonds, green chiles, garlic, and ginger in a high-speed blender to a paste, adding a little water if necessary to make it smooth.

3. In a bowl, mix together the yogurt, ground cumin, ground coriander, garam masala, and salt, then add the onion paste and mix well.

4. Pour the marinade over the lamb and, using your hands, massage all over, making sure to push the marinade into the slits and coating the lamb well. Cover with plastic wrap and refrigerate for 2–3 hours, or overnight.

5. Remove the lamb from the refrigerator and allow to come up to room temperature. Preheat the oven to 425°F.

6. Heat the oil in a frying pan over medium heat. Add the bay leaves, cassia, cardamom, peppercorns, and cloves and fry for 30 seconds, or until slightly changed in color.

7. Pour the spices over the marinated meat, add a splash of water, and cover tightly with foil.

8. Place the lamb in the oven for up to 4 hours, or until the meat falls away from the bone, reducing the heat to 250°F after the first 30 minutes. Uncover the lamb after the first 2 hours.

9. Let the lamb rest for 15–20 minutes. Garnish with lemon wedges, if you like.

Mussels in Chile, Ginger, and Curry Leaf Broth

MAKE SURE YOU HAVE PLENTY OF CRUSTY BREAD TO HELP SOAK UP
THE SPICY COCONUT AND GINGER BROTH, WHICH IS FULL OF
FLAVOR AND WORKS EXTREMELY WELL WITH MUSSELS.

SERVES 4 | PREPARATION TIME: 20 MINUTES | COOKING TIME: 5 MINUTES

FRESH
7 garlic cloves, finely sliced
12 fresh curry leaves
4-inch piece ginger, peeled and cut into julienne
2 lb large mussels, scrubbed and debearded if necessary

SPICES
2 whole dried chiles
3 teaspoons garam masala
1 teaspoon ground turmeric

PANTRY
4 tablespoons oil
6 tablespoons vegetable stock
½ cup light coconut milk
Salt, to taste

GARNISH
1 lime, cut into wedges
1 tablespoon finely chopped cilantro

SERVE
Mint Parantha (page 118)

1. Heat the oil in a large, heavy pan over medium-low heat. Add the dried chiles, garlic, and curry leaves and fry until lightly golden.

2. Turn the heat down, add the garam masala and turmeric and stir-fry for 30 seconds.

3. Next, add the ginger and fry for a further 1 minute. Add the mussels, discarding any that do not close to the touch, and toss around until well coated.

4. Add the stock, coconut milk, and salt, cover, and simmer for 3–4 minutes, or until the mussels have opened. Discard any mussels that remain closed.

5. Garnish with lime wedges and cilantro and serve with Mint Parantha.

Chicken Korma

CONSIDERED TO BE A GENTLE INTRODUCTION TO INDIAN CUISINE FOR
WESTERNERS, CHICKEN KORMA IS A MILD YET VERY FLAVORSOME DISH.
AS IT'S NOT SPICY, CONSIDER SERVING THIS TO CHILDREN. IT GOES
WELL WITH AROMATIC RICE, SALAD, AND NAAN BREAD (PAGE 127).

SERVES 4–5 | PREPARATION TIME: 2 HOURS | MARINATING TIME: 2–8 HOURS
COOKING TIME: 30–60 MINUTES

FRESH

1¾ lb bone-in chicken pieces

⅔ cup (5 oz) plain yogurt

4 garlic cloves, minced

1 tablespoon lemon juice

2 onions, roughly chopped

2-inch piece ginger, peeled and roughly chopped

1–2 small green chiles, roughly chopped

SPICES

3 bay leaves

12 green cardamom pods, cracked

1½ teaspoons ground coriander

½ teaspoon ground turmeric

PANTRY

6 tablespoons oil

2 tablespoons cashews and 1 tablespoon white poppy seeds, soaked together in ¼ cup hot water

1½ teaspoons salt, or to taste

Hot water, as needed

3 tablespoons heavy cream

GARNISH

Large pinch of ground cumin

1. Make slits in each chicken piece, place in a large bowl, and add 4 tablespoons of the yogurt, 2 teaspoons of the garlic, 1 tablespoon of the oil, and the lemon juice. Mix thoroughly until well coated. Cover and chill for 2 hours, or overnight.

2. In a blender, blitz the soaked cashews and poppy seeds with their soaking water, then transfer to a bowl and mix with the remaining yogurt.

3. Heat the remaining oil in a large, heavy pan over medium heat. Add the onions, remaining garlic, ginger, and chiles and fry until soft and golden brown. Transfer with a slotted spoon to the blender and blitz together to a smooth paste.

4. Pour the paste back into the same pan, add the bay leaves and cardamom and fry together over medium-low heat for 2–3 minutes.

5. Add the ground coriander, turmeric, and salt and stir-fry for 1 minute.

6. Next, add the cashew and yogurt paste and continue stir-frying for a further 2 minutes.

7. Add the chicken pieces and stir-fry for 5–6 minutes, adding a little hot water to loosen if needed, add the cream, then cover and cook for a further 15–20 minutes, or until cooked through.

8. Garnish with a sprinkling of ground cumin.

Classic Lamb Curry

ANOTHER FAVORITE DISH HAILING FROM NORTH INDIA, THIS IS PERFECT FOR ANY OCCASION AND HITS THE RIGHT SPOT FOR ALL CURRY LOVERS. THIS DISH IS SIMPLE, YET RICH IN FLAVOR AND, LIKE MOST CURRIES, TASTES EVEN BETTER THE NEXT DAY.

SERVES 4 | PREPARATION TIME: 30 MINUTES | COOKING TIME: 45 MINUTES

FRESH

3 onions, finely chopped

2 small green chiles

1½-inch piece ginger, peeled and finely grated

8 garlic cloves, finely chopped

2 lb leg of lamb, chopped into 1-inch cubes

2 tablespoons Greek yogurt, whisked with 1 scant cup water

3 tablespoons finely chopped cilantro

SPICES

1 tablespoon garam masala

1½ teaspoons ground cumin, plus a large pinch for sprinkling

1½ teaspoons ground coriander

½ teaspoon chile powder

1 tablespoon ground turmeric

PANTRY

3 tablespoons oil

4 oz canned diced tomatoes

2 teaspoons salt, or to taste

1. In a blender or using a mortar and pestle, grind the onions, green chiles, ginger, garlic, oil, and canned tomatoes into a smooth paste.

2. Mix the paste together with the garam masala, cumin, coriander, chile powder, turmeric, and salt. Place the lamb in a large bowl and cover with the spice paste, making sure all the pieces of lamb are well coated.

3. Put the lamb into a heavy saucepan over low heat, cover, and cook for 35–40 minutes, stirring frequently, until the meat is tender and the oil has separated.

4. Add the yogurt, then cover and cook for a further 5 minutes, stirring constantly over medium-low heat.

5. Remove from the heat and sprinkle with the chopped cilantro and a large pinch of ground cumin, then serve.

Lemon and Saffron Pot Roast Chicken

A DELICIOUS, LAID-BACK DISH BEST ENJOYED WITH FRIENDS AT LUNCH.
SERVE WITH STEAMED GREEN BEANS IN TOMATO AND MUSTARD DRESSING
(PAGE 74), A SIMPLE SALAD, AND STEAMED POTATOES.

SERVES 3–4 | PREPARATION TIME: 15 MINUTES | COOKING TIME: 1½ HOURS

FRESH

2 tablespoons grated ginger

3 garlic cloves, finely chopped

Zest and juice of 2 lemons

3 lb whole chicken

2 tablespoons crème fraîche

SPICES

1 tablespoon ground cumin

2 tablespoons ground coriander

5–6 saffron threads,
soaked in 1 teaspoon milk
(see Saffron Essence, page 228)

BOUQUET GARNI SPICES

1 large cinnamon stick

2 bay leaves

3 star anise

4 cardamom pods

PANTRY

2–3 tablespoons vegetable oil

2 teaspoons salt, or to taste

1. Preheat the oven to 375°F.

2. Place the ginger, garlic, ground cumin, ground coriander, lemon zest and juice, soaked saffron threads, and oil in a bowl and mix. Rub all over the whole chicken and place in a lidded ovenproof dish.

3. Add the bouquet garni spices and salt, then pour in enough water to come a third of the way up the chicken. Cover with the lid.

4. Place in the oven and cook for 1 hour, then remove the lid and cook for a further 15–25 minutes, or until the chicken is cooked through.

5. Remove the chicken from the dish, then pour half of the cooking stock into a pan and stir in the crème fraîche. Place over low heat and simmer for 10–15 minutes, or until the sauce has reduced and slightly thickened.

6. Cut the chicken into serving pieces and pour over the sauce.

NOTE: The spices can be added straight into the dish instead of making a bouquet garni.

Salmon Baked with Crème Fraîche and Coconut

Kindly shared by unconventional cook Jeeva Jeyaseelan, this recipe is a simple preparation that is packed full of flavor but still delicate. The crème fraîche, lime juice, and coconut all together form a delicious and light sauce that works well with any fish, either fillets or as whole fish for more people.

SERVES 2 | PREPARATION TIME: 15 MINUTES | COOKING TIME: 15 MINUTES

FRESH

1 recipe Spiced Coconut and Crème Fraîche Marinade (page 246)

2 salmon fillets

¼ wedge of lime

PANTRY

2 large sheets (8½ x 11 inches) parchment paper

1. Preheat the oven to 350°F.

2. Rub the marinade equally into the pieces of salmon.

3. Place one salmon fillet on each parchment sheet, then squeeze lime juice over each piece and finish off by sprinkling 2–3 teaspoons water over each fillet.

4. Bring up the sides of the paper and pinch together, then seal the edges tightly to form a loose parcel.

5. Place both salmon parcels on a baking sheet and cook in the oven for 12–15 minutes, depending on the thickness of the fillets.

NOTE: Open the parcels very carefully, as the steam that will escape will be very hot. Any leftovers can be made into mouthwatering fish cakes.

Lamb Kofta and Saffron Crème Fraîche

THIS IS A TRADITIONAL NORTH INDIAN DISH, USUALLY MADE WITH LAMB, BUT YOU CAN ALSO CONSIDER USING BEEF, WHICH IS EQUALLY AS NICE. PREPARE THE MEATBALLS AND THE SAUCE SEPARATELY THE NIGHT BEFORE. THE NEXT DAY, COMBINE AND FINISH OFF COOKING ACCORDING TO THE RECIPE. THE DELICIOUS SAFFRON-INFUSED CRÈME FRAÎCHE GARNISH IS AN OPTIONAL EXTRA, BUT GIVES THE DISH A LUXURIOUS FINISH.

SERVES 4 | PREPARATION TIME: 2 HOURS
CHILLING TIME: 1–8 HOURS | COOKING TIME: ABOUT 1½ HOURS

FRESH
1 lb ground lamb
2 onions, grated and squeezed dry with a cloth
8 garlic cloves, minced
3 tablespoons grated ginger
4 small green chiles
4 tablespoons finely chopped cilantro

SPICES
2 teaspoons cumin seeds
4 black cardamom pods, cracked
2 bay leaves
1-inch cassia or cinnamon stick
1 tablespoon garam masala
1 teaspoon ground turmeric
Large pinch of nutmeg

PANTRY
4 tablespoons oil
1 teaspoon salt, plus more to taste
2 tablespoons tomato purée dissolved in 1 cup hot water or meat stock

OPTIONAL GARNISH
Tiny pinch of saffron threads, soaked in 1 tablespoon hot water, then mixed together with 1–2 tablespoons crème fraîche and 1 tablespoon lemon juice

1. Add the following to a large high-speed blender: half of the onions, garlic, ginger, and cilantro. Add the lamb and 2 chiles, 1 teaspoon salt, and blitz together until completely smooth. You may need to stop the blender, remove the lid, and move the mixture around with a spatula.

2. Put the mixture in a large bowl and, using damp hands, roll a small portion of the mixture into a smooth ball. Place the ball onto a lightly oiled sheet pan. Repeat with the remaining mixture, cover with plastic wrap, and refrigerate for 1–2 hours, or preferably overnight.

3. Heat the oil in a heavy pan over medium-low heat. Add the cumin seeds, cardamom pods, bay leaves, and cassia and fry for 20 seconds.

4. Next, reduce the heat slightly and add the remaining onions, garlic, ginger, cilantro, and chiles and fry for 5 minutes, or until golden brown.

5. Add the garam masala, turmeric, and nutmeg, season with salt, and keep stirring and frying for 30 seconds.

6. Pour in the tomato purée mixture, bring to a gentle simmer, then gently slip in the meatballs and continue cooking, uncovered, for a further 30–35 minutes, or until the meatballs are cooked through and the sauce is thick. Drizzle with the crème fraîche garnish, if using.

Fish in Tamarind Sauce

THE TAMARIND IN THIS GRAVY-BASED DISH GIVES IT A LOVELY
TANGY FLAVOR THAT GOES REALLY WELL WITH SIMPLE, PLAIN BOILED
RICE AND RAW SHREDDED VEGETABLE SALAD OR STEAMED GREENS.

SERVES 4–5 | PREPARATION TIME: 30 MINUTES
MARINATING TIME: 1 HOUR | COOKING TIME: 40 MINUTES

FRESH

5 pieces fish, such as halibut, cod, or
haddock, each 1 inch thick

1 recipe Coconut and Tamarind with
Red Chile and Ground Spices
Marinade (page 247)

8–10 fresh curry leaves

2 green chiles, slit lengthwise
down the middle

2 onions, roughly chopped

3 garlic cloves and ½-inch piece ginger,
mashed into a paste (see page 231)

1 large tomato, finely chopped

SPICES

1½ teaspoons black mustard seeds

½ teaspoon ground cumin

PANTRY

3 tablespoons vegetable oil

Salt and black pepper, to taste

1 cup (8 oz) canned coconut milk

1. Put the pieces of fish in a large, flat dish and mix in the marinade, making sure all the pieces are well coated. Cover and marinate for 1 hour.

2. Heat the oil in a deep pan over medium heat until hot. Add the curry leaves, black mustard seeds, and green chiles and fry until the crackling stops.

3. Now add the onions and the garlic and ginger paste and fry over low heat until the paste begins to brown very slightly, about 6–8 minutes.

4. Add the chopped tomato and fry, stirring frequently, over low heat for 3–4 minutes, or until the onion base starts to release its oil and turns a rich golden brown.

5. Lift out the fish and set aside. Add the fish marinade to the pan and stir. Gently bring to a boil over medium heat and add pepper, the cumin, and coconut milk. Turn down the heat slightly and simmer until the oil begins to appear on top of the gravy. Add the fish now and cook for 12–15 minutes, or until the fish flakes easily with a fork. If stirring, do so very gently to avoid breaking the fish.

Beef and Potato Curry

A SLOW-SIMMERED CURRY WITH AN INTERESTING COMBINATION OF SPICES
IS JUST THE THING TO WARM YOU UP ON A WINTRY DAY. SERVE WITH WARMED
NAAN BREAD (PAGE 127) AND SPINACH AND MINT YOGURT (PAGE 196).
THIS DISH IS PERFECT FOR MEAT LOVERS AND CAN BE ENJOYED
DURING A CASUAL DINNER PARTY OR A FAMILY MEAL.

SERVES 4 | PREPARATION TIME: 35 MINUTES | COOKING TIME: 2 HOURS 10 MINUTES

FRESH

3 onions, finely chopped

8 small green chiles, finely chopped

1-inch piece ginger, peeled and finely shredded

4 garlic cloves, minced

2 lb stewing beef, diced into 1-inch cubes

1 potato, peeled and chopped into large cubes

SPICES

1½ tablespoons garam masala

1 tablespoon ground turmeric

4 cloves

2 bay leaves

4 green cardamom pods, slightly cracked

2-inch cassia or cinnamon stick, or 1 teaspoon ground cinnamon

1 teaspoon fennel seeds

PANTRY

13.5-oz can coconut milk

¼ cup ground almonds

1 tablespoon tomato purée

3 tablespoons ghee or oil

2 teaspoons salt, or to taste

1. Mix together the coconut milk, ground almonds, and tomato purée to form a paste. Set aside.

2. In a mini blender or using a mortar and pestle, grind the onions, green chiles, garam masala, turmeric, ginger, and garlic to a smooth paste.

3. Heat the ghee in a large, heavy pan over medium heat. Add the cloves, bay leaves, cardamom, cassia, and fennel seeds and fry for 1 minute.

4. When they begin to crackle, add the onion paste and cook over low heat for 3–4 minutes, or until the oil separates and the paste turns golden brown.

5. Stir in the meat, turn up the heat slightly, and continue cooking, stirring occasionally, for 10–12 minutes, or until the liquid has evaporated and the meat starts to brown.

6. Next, stir in the coconut paste and salt, then stir well until the meat is coated. Cook for 4–5 minutes, stirring occasionally. Cover and simmer for about 1¼ hours.

7. Add the potato, cover, and continue simmering for 30 minutes, or until the meat is tender and the potato cooked through.

8. Remove from the heat, cover, and let the meat rest for 15–20 minutes before serving.

Prawn Curry

DELIGHTFUL, WITH A KICK, THIS SOUTH INDIAN PRAWN-LOVER'S FAVORITE
DISH IS IDEAL FOR COLD WINTER EVENINGS OR LIGHT SUMMER SUPPERS.

SERVES 4 | PREPARATION TIME: 20 MINUTES | COOKING TIME: 15 MINUTES

FRESH

1 lb fresh prawns

Juice of 1 lime

7–8 fresh curry leaves

½ onion, finely chopped

3 garlic cloves, finely crushed

2 teaspoons grated ginger

Juice of ½ lemon

SPICES

2-inch cassia or cinnamon stick

½ teaspoon fenugreek seeds

½ teaspoon ground turmeric

1 teaspoon chile powder

PANTRY

3 tablespoons oil

¼ cup (2 oz) creamed coconut

1 teaspoon salt, or to taste

1. Shell and devein the prawns. Put them into a bowl, add the lime juice and leave to stand for 5 minutes. Wash the prawns under cold water and pat dry with paper towels.

2. Heat the oil in a medium saucepan, then reduce the heat and add the cassia and curry leaves. Toss around for a few seconds, then add the fenugreek seeds and fry for a further 1 minute, or until the seeds are a rich dark brown.

3. Add the onion and fry over medium heat until golden brown. Next, add the garlic and ginger and fry for a further 1 minute.

4. Turn the heat down, add the turmeric and fry for a further 1 minute. Next, add the creamed coconut, chile powder, ½ cup water, and salt. Bring slowly to a boil, then reduce the heat and simmer until the creamed coconut has dissolved.

5. Add the prawns, bring back to a boil, then reduce the heat and simmer for 5–7 minutes.

6. Finally, remove the pan from the heat, add the lemon juice, and mix thoroughly.

NOTE: If using precooked prawns, add them to the simmering sauce just prior to serving.

Butter Chicken

CREATED IN A POPULAR EATING JOINT IN THE BACK STREETS OF DELHI
OVER 40 YEARS AGO, BUTTER CHICKEN NOW HAS AN ICONIC STATUS
IN INDIA AS THE FAVORITE NONVEGETARIAN CHOICE. INDULGE YOURSELF IN
THIS RICH AND FLAVORSOME TREAT THAT GOES WELL WITH
NAAN BREAD (PAGE 127) AS WELL AS AROMATIC RICE.

SERVES 4 | PREPARATION TIME: 30 MINUTES | COOKING TIME: 20 MINUTES

FRESH

2 onions, roughly chopped

4 garlic cloves, roughly chopped

2-inch piece ginger, peeled
and roughly chopped

14 oz Chicken Tikka (page 48) or skinless,
boneless chicken thighs (see Note)

2 tablespoons heavy cream

1 recipe cooked Simple Plain Rice
(page 134)

SPICES

2 black cardamom pods,
slightly cracked

4 green cardamom pods,
slightly cracked

1 teaspoon ground turmeric

1 teaspoon garam masala

½–1 teaspoon chile powder

PANTRY

4 tablespoons oil

1 teaspoon salt, or to taste

2 tablespoons tomato purée

2 tablespoons coconut milk powder

1 tablespoon ground almonds

¼ teaspoon granulated sugar

1 teaspoon melted ghee, for drizzling

1. Heat 2 tablespoons of the oil in a pan over medium heat. Add the onions, garlic, and ginger and fry for 3–4 minutes, or until caramelized and golden brown. Remove from the heat, let cool slightly, then blitz into a smooth paste in a blender.

2. Add the remaining oil to the same pan and heat over medium heat. Add the black and green cardamom pods and gently fry for 30 seconds, then straight away add the onion paste.

3. Turn the heat down and add the turmeric, garam masala, chile powder, and salt and stir-fry for 1 minute, then remove from the heat.

4. Next, blitz together the tomato purée, coconut milk powder, ground almonds, sugar, and ¼ cup water in the blender. Pour into the pan and stir. Return the pan to low heat and cook for 3–5 minutes. Add the cooked chicken pieces and heat through gently for 3–4 minutes. Add the heavy cream and cook for a further 2 minutes.

5. Finish off with a drizzle of ghee and serve with Simple Plain Rice.

NOTE: Cubed raw chicken thighs can also be used; cover and increase the cooking time to 20 minutes.

breads and rice

CHAPTER 4

Mint Parantha

This refreshing twist on the plain parantha goes well with flavored yogurts, meat, or vegetable dishes. As with all paranthas, they are best eaten hot.

MAKES 6–8 | PREPARATION TIME: 45 MINUTES
COOKING TIME: 3–4 MINUTES PER PARANTHA

FRESH
1 bunch (3 oz) mint leaves, finely chopped
1 recipe Plain Naan dough (page 127)

SPICES
2 teaspoons ground cumin
1 teaspoon ground black pepper
¼ teaspoon ajwain seeds (optional)

PANTRY
½ teaspoon salt, or to taste
Flour, for dusting
¼ cup melted ghee, butter, or oil
1 tablespoon dried mint

OPTIONAL GARNISH
Chaat masala

1. Heat a flat griddle or nonstick frying pan over medium-low heat.

2. Using a mortar and pestle, pound together the mint leaves, cumin, pepper, salt, and ajwain seeds, if using. Set aside.

3. Lightly dust the work surface with flour. Divide the dough into 6–8 equal pieces. Flatten one piece and dust with flour. Using a rolling pin, roll it into a circle with a 5-inch diameter. Use a brush to spread some melted ghee all over the circle and sprinkle with flour.

4. Take a heaping teaspoon of the mint spice mix and spread all over the circle of dough.

5. Starting from one side, fold and gather the dough together like a fan, then curl up from one side and roll back into a ball. Press down and dust with flour. Roll out until it becomes a large thin circle. If sticking in between, keep dusting with flour. Repeat with the remaining dough circles and spice mix.

6. Gently lift the parantha off the work surface and place onto the hot pan. Turn up the heat to medium. The parantha will soon start to puff up. After 30 seconds, flip over, brush very lightly with water, and sprinkle a pinch of dried mint all over. Gently press using a spatula, cook for 1 minute, flip again, and brush with melted ghee. Flip over again and swirl around the pan for 30 seconds. Brush with more ghee and serve hot, sprinkled with chaat masala, if you like.

NOTE: If made in advance, gently reheat each one in a frying pan before serving.

Parantha with Ajwain, Fennel, and Chile

PARANTHAS ARE USUALLY EATEN AS PART OF BREAKFAST OR BRUNCH,
SERVED WITH MASALA SCRAMBLED EGGS (PAGE 70) AND
ACCOMPANIED WITH A GLASS OF HOT MASALA CHAI (PAGE 212).

MAKES 6–8 | PREPARATION TIME: 45 MINUTES
COOKING TIME: 3–4 MINUTES PER PARANTHA

FRESH

1 recipe Plain Roti dough
(page 126)

SPICES

¼ teaspoon ajwain seeds

¼ teaspoon fennel seeds

¼ teaspoon red pepper flakes

PANTRY

½ teaspoon salt, or to taste

Flour, for dusting

2 tablespoons melted ghee

1. Heat a flat griddle or nonstick frying pan over medium-low heat.

2. Using a mortar and pestle, crush together the ajwain and fennel seeds, red pepper flakes, and salt and set aside.

3. Lightly dust the work surface with flour. Divide the dough into 6–8 equal pieces, then roll dough balls between the palms of your hands and flatten into discs. Dust with flour and, using a rolling pin, roll each into a circle with a 5-inch diameter. Use a brush to spread some melted ghee all over each circle.

4. Take a couple of large pinches of the spice mix and sprinkle liberally all over a dough circle. Bring one side of the circle into the middle and press lightly. Spread a little ghee over the top, fold the opposite side of the rolled dough on top of the folded part, then press lightly and brush with melted ghee. Lastly, fold the top and bottom parts and brush with a little more ghee. Dust the small square with flour and roll out until it becomes a large thin square. If sticking in between, keep dusting with flour. Repeat with the remaining dough circles and spice mix.

5. Gently lift the parantha off the work surface and place onto the hot pan. Turn up the heat to medium. The parantha will soon start to puff up. After 30–60 seconds flip over and gently press with a spatula. Cook for 1 minute, flip again and brush with ghee, then flip over again and swirl around the pan for 30 seconds. Serve hot.

NOTE: To make plain paranthas, leave out the spice mix and use only the salt.

White Radish and Onion Parantha

These "all-in-one" breads do take some effort and a little skill, but they are worth it. The bread envelops the spiced daikon masala, leaving it tender and sweet. Perfect for brunch or a picnic, they are delicious hot, and still fantastic served cold.

MAKES 6–8 | PREPARATION TIME: 1 HOUR
COOKING TIME: 3–5 MINUTES PER PARANTHA

FRESH

8 oz daikon, finely shredded into long ribbons and squeezed dry with a cloth

½ small red onion, finely chopped and squeezed dry with a cloth

½ green chile, finely chopped

1-inch piece ginger, peeled and finely shredded or chopped

2 tablespoons finely chopped cilantro

1 recipe Plain Roti dough (page 126)

SPICES

½ teaspoon pomegranate seed powder

½ teaspoon ajwain seeds

1 tablespoon fenugreek leaves

1 teaspoon garam masala

1 teaspoon ground cumin

PANTRY

Flour, for dusting

1 teaspoon salt, or to taste

1. Mix together the daikon, onion, chile, ginger, cilantro, pomegranate powder, ajwain seeds, fenugreek leaves, garam masala, and ground cumin in a bowl.

2. Heat a flat griddle or heavy nonstick frying pan or crêpe pan over medium-low heat.

3. Divide the dough into 6–8 equal pieces, then roll into balls between the palms of your hands and flatten into small discs. Dust the discs with flour and, using a rolling pin, roll out until they become medium-size discs. If sticking in between, keep dusting with flour.

4. Take 1 heaping tablespoon of the daikon mixture and place in the middle of a disc. Sprinkle with a large pinch of salt, then bring together the sides and pinch in the middle until the mixture is completely concealed. Dust with flour, flatten, and continue to gently roll out to a large thin disc. Repeat with all the discs and filling.

5. Gently lift the parantha off the work surface and place onto the hot pan. Turn up the heat to medium. The parantha will soon start to puff up. After 30–60 seconds, flip over. Gently press the parantha using a spatula, cook for 1 minute, and flip again. Brush with ghee, then flip over again and swirl around the pan for 30 seconds. Serve hot or cold.

Cauliflower, Cumin, and Green Onion Parantha

CRISPY PARANTHA STUFFED WITH FINELY SHREDDED CAULIFLOWER, TOASTED CUMIN, AND GREEN ONION IS A SUBSTANTIAL CHOICE FOR BRUNCH, LUNCH, OR AS A SNACK. SERVE WITH PLAIN YOGURT SPRINKLED WITH A PINCH OF CHAAT MASALA.

MAKES 6–8 | PREPARATION TIME: 1 HOUR
COOKING TIME: 3–5 MINUTES PER PARANTHA

FRESH

5 oz cauliflower, finely grated or blitzed in high-speed blender until fine

2 green onions, finely sliced

¾-inch piece ginger, peeled and finely grated

½ small red chile, seeded if you like and finely chopped

2 tablespoons finely chopped cilantro

1 recipe Plain Roti dough (page 126)

SPICES

1 teaspoon cumin seeds, toasted and finely crushed

1 teaspoon garam masala

¾ tablespoon fenugreek leaves

PANTRY

1 teaspoon salt, or to taste

Flour, for dusting

1. Mix together the cauliflower, green onions, ginger, chile, cilantro, cumin seeds, garam masala, and fenugreek leaves.

2. Heat a flat griddle, heavy nonstick frying pan, or crêpe pan over medium-low heat.

3. Divide the dough into 6–8 equal pieces, then roll into balls between the palms of your hands and flatten into small discs. Dust the discs with flour and, using a rolling pin, roll out to medium-sized discs. If sticking in between, keep dusting with flour.

4. Take 1 heaping tablespoon of the cauliflower mixture and place in the middle of a disc, sprinkle with a little salt, then bring together the sides and pinch in the middle until the mixture is completely concealed. Dust with flour, flatten, and continue to gently roll out to a large thin disc. Repeat with all the discs and filling.

5. Gently lift the parantha off the work surface and place onto the hot pan. Turn up the heat to medium. The parantha will soon start to puff up. After 30–60 seconds, flip over. Gently press the parantha using a spatula and cook for 1 minute. Flip again and brush with ghee, then flip over again and swirl around the pan for 30 seconds. Serve hot.

HOW TO MAKE
Plain Roti

ROTI IS AN EVERYDAY INDIAN FLATBREAD, WHEREAS NAAN IS THE MOST
POPULAR FLATBREAD, ESPECIALLY OUTSIDE OF INDIA. ROTI IS THINNER,
CONTAINS NO YEAST, AND IS COOKED ON A FLAT GRIDDLE PAN.

MAKES 6–8 | PREPARATION TIME: 20–25 MINUTES | RESTING TIME: 20–25 MINUTES
COOKING TIME: 2 MINUTES EACH SIDE

EQUIPMENT

LARGE BOWL
MEASURING CUP
ROLLING PIN
FLAT GRIDDLE PAN
PASTRY BRUSH

sift

mix

1 Sift 2½ cups whole-wheat, atta, or chapati flour or 1½ cups self-rising flour into a large bowl.

2 Drizzle 1 tablespoon oil over the flour and make a well in the center. Using one hand, pour in ½ cup cold water, a little at a time, and with the other hand use a fork to gradually bring in the flour and mix together. Keep pouring a little water, while mixing and kneading together. Add enough water to make a soft, but not sticky dough. If it's too wet, add more flour; if too dry, add more water.

rest

3 Keep kneading for about 5 minutes, or until the dough is smooth, pliable and soft. The consistency should be neither very soft nor hard. Cover and let rest for 20–25 minutes.

4 Divide the dough into 6–8 equal-sized pieces, then roll the balls in the palms of your hands. Using a rolling pin, roll each one out into a thin, large disc.

cook

roll

5 Gently lift and place onto a hot griddle. Cook one side until half-cooked, flip over using tongs, and cook until brown spots appear. Flip back over and finish the other side until the roti starts to puff up. Remove and brush with some ghee or butter. Serve hot.

HOW TO MAKE
Plain Naan

NAAN IS AN UNLEAVENED BREAD MADE USING YEAST. IT IS SOFT, LIGHT, AND TRADITIONALLY MADE IN CLAY OVENS. BOTH NAAN AND ROTI MAKE A PERFECT CHOICE FOR WRAPS AND ACCOMPANIMENT FOR CURRIES.

MAKES 7–8 | PREPARATION TIME: 1 HOUR | RESTING TIME: 20–25 MINUTES
COOKING TIME: 2–3 MINUTES EACH SIDE

EQUIPMENT

LARGE BOWL
MEASURING CUP
BAKING SHEET
ROLLING PIN
PASTRY BRUSH

1

Mix together a ¼-oz packet dried yeast, 1 teaspoon golden superfine sugar (optional), and 1 scant cup warm water. Stir well with a fork and leave for a few minutes. Place 2¾ cups bread flour, 2 tablespoons melted ghee or oil, and ¼ tablespoon fine sea salt into a wide bowl and make a well in the center.

stir

2

Using one hand, pour in a little of the yeast mixture, and with the other hand use a fork to gradually bring the flour in and mix together. Keep pouring a little of the yeast mixture while mixing. Flour your hands and begin to knead and form a ball. Add enough of the yeast mixture to make a soft, but not sticky dough and keep kneading for about 5 minutes, or until smooth, pliable, and soft. The consistency should be neither very soft nor hard. Cover and let rest for 20–25 minutes.

mix

3

Using lightly oiled hands, divide the dough into about 7–8 equal-sized balls. Place on a lightly oiled baking sheet, leaving gaps in between the balls, and cover with a damp kitchen towel. Leave in a warm place until the balls have doubled in size, about 20 minutes.

divide

4

Preheat the broiler with a heavy-duty baking sheet or broiler pan placed on the top rack. Roll out the dough balls thinly and evenly. One by one, place the rolled-out naan onto the baking sheet, brush lightly with water, and broil for 1–2 minutes on both sides, or until lightly browned and puffed up. Lightly brush with some ghee and serve hot.

bake

Seeded Naan Bread

THE MIXED SEEDS IN THIS RECIPE BRING THE NAAN BREAD ALIVE.
ALSO TRY KNEADING WITH BLACK POPPY SEEDS, FENUGREEK LEAVES,
DRIED FRUIT, OR FINELY CHOPPED NUTS. A TEARDROP OR LEAF SHAPE
IS MOST COMMON, BUT ROLL OUT IN ANY SHAPE YOU LIKE.

MAKES 8–10 | PREPARATION TIME: ABOUT 1 HOUR
COOKING TIME: 4–5 MINUTES PER NAAN

FRESH
1 recipe Plain Naan dough
(page 127)

SPICES
1 teaspoon fennel seeds
1 teaspoon caraway seeds
¼ teaspoon ajwain seeds (optional)
½ tablespoon sesame seeds
½ tablespoon nigella seeds

PANTRY
Melted ghee, for brushing

1. Using a mortar and pestle or using a rolling pin, lightly crush together the fennel, caraway, and ajwain seeds, if using, and add to the dry flour for Plain Naan (see step 1, page 127).

2. Follow the steps for the Plain Naan recipe, but just before placing under the broiler, sprinkle each naan with a large pinch each of the sesame and nigella seeds. Continue according to the Plain Naan recipe. Brush lightly with ghee and serve hot.

NOTE: These naans freeze very well. Cook, but don't brush with butter or sprinkle with seeds. Freeze with parchment paper in between in a plastic freezer bag for up to 1 month.

Mixed Vegetable Roti

UNLIKE STUFFED PARANTHAS, THIS RECIPE SIMPLY KNEADS TOGETHER
SHREDDED VEGETABLES AND SPICES. CONSIDER USING SHREDDED
CELERY, BROCCOLI, CABBAGE, DAIKON, OR POTATOES.

SERVES 6–8 | PREPARATION TIME: 1 HOUR
RESTING TIME: 20–25 MINUTES | COOKING TIME: 3–4 MINUTES PER ROTI

FRESH

5 oz carrots (2 medium), roughly chopped

5 oz cauliflower, roughly chopped

4 oz spinach, roughly chopped

½ leek, roughly chopped

1-inch piece ginger, peeled and roughly chopped

½ small green chile, seeded if you like and finely sliced

2 tablespoons roughly chopped cilantro

1 recipe Plain Roti dough (page 126)

SPICES

1 teaspoon sesame seeds

½ teaspoon ajwain seeds

¼ teaspoon ground turmeric

1½ teaspoons garam masala

1 tablespoon fenugreek leaves

PANTRY

1 teaspoon salt, or to taste

Flour, for dusting

2 tablespoons melted ghee, for brushing

1. Place the carrots, cauliflower, spinach, leek, green chile, and cilantro into a high-speed blender and pulse until finely shredded and mixed together.

2. Add the mixture to the flour for Plain Roti (see step 1, page 126). Mix and massage the shredded vegetables with the flour, and add the sesame seeds, ajwain seeds, turmeric, garam masala, fenugreek leaves, and salt until all the water from the vegetables has been soaked up by the flour, then gradually start adding the water (see step 2) and bring the dough together. Keep kneading to form a soft and smooth consistency, then let the dough rest for 20–25 minutes.

3. Heat a heavy nonstick frying pan or crêpe pan over medium-low heat. Divide the dough into 6–8 equal pieces, then roll dough balls between the palms of your hands. Using a rolling pin, roll each one out into a thin large disc. Add a dusting of flour if sticking.

4. Gently lift each disc and place onto the hot pan. Cook one side until a little less than half-cooked, then flip over with tongs and cook until brown spots appear. Flip back over and finish cooking the other side until the roti starts to puff up. Remove from the pan and brush with ghee. Serve hot.

Onion and Cilantro Stuffed Naan

EAT THIS SOFT NAAN BREAD STUFFED WITH ONION AND FRESH CILANTRO ALONGSIDE
MASALA-BASED DISHES, SKEWERED MEATS, OR BARBECUED PANEER.

MAKES 8–10 | PREPARATION TIME: ABOUT 30 MINUTES
COOKING TIME: 4–5 MINUTES PER NAAN

FRESH

1 small red onion, finely grated
and squeezed dry with a cloth

3–4 tablespoons finely
chopped cilantro

1 recipe Plain Naan dough
(page 127)

SPICES

¼ teaspoon red pepper flakes
(optional)

PANTRY

Salt, to taste

Flour, for dusting

4 tablespoons melted ghee

1. Preheat the broiler, with a heavy baking sheet placed
on the top rack.

2. In a bowl, mix together the red onion, cilantro, red
pepper flakes, if using, and salt.

3. Divide the Plain Naan dough into 8–10 equal pieces
and roll into balls between the palms of your hands. Roll
out the dough balls thinly and evenly. Place a small heap
of the onion and cilantro mixture in the center of each one,
leaving the edges free.

4. Pinch the edges of the dough together all the way
around to form a pouch, then flip the pouch so the seam
side is facing down on a well-floured surface. Flour the top
and roll the pouch into an oval ⅛ inch thick. Add a dusting
of flour if sticking.

5. Place the rolled-out naan on the baking sheet, brush
lightly with water, and broil for 1–2 minutes on both sides,
or until lightly browned and puffed up.

6. Brush the naan with melted ghee and serve hot.

Simple Plain Rice

MAKE PERFECT WHITE RICE EVERY TIME WITH THIS RECIPE. THEN TRY THE
NEXT STEP IF YOU WISH — ADD MORE FLAVOR BY TEMPERING THE RICE,
SAUTÉING IT IN SPICE-INFUSED OIL, OR COOK IT WITH A BOUQUET GARNI OR
FLAVORED STOCK. ALWAYS TASTE THE RICE TO CHECK FOR DONENESS.

SERVES 4 | PREPARATION TIME: 5 MINUTES | COOKING TIME: 20 MINUTES

PANTRY

1 cup basmati rice,
thoroughly washed

2 cups hot water

½ teaspoon salt, or to taste

2 teaspoons ghee (optional)

1. In a medium saucepan with a tight-fitting lid, mix the rice, hot water, and salt and bring to a boil. Gently stir once, cover with the lid, and reduce the heat to low. Simmer for about 18 minutes.

2. Keep the lid on and remove the pan from the heat. Leave to stand covered for a further 5 minutes. Fluff up with a fork and gently stir in the ghee, if using, before serving.

NOTE: If you need to make a different quantity of rice, always use 1 measure of dry rice to 2 measures of water.

Khichadi

This is wholesome comfort food — a bulked-up version of a humble dish that's usually eaten more soupy, with only a pinch of salt and black pepper and no dairy or spices. It is mainly served to calm, heal, and soothe the digestive system when one is not well. This recipe has more of a risotto texture.

SERVES 4 | PREPARATION TIME: 25 MINUTES | COOKING TIME: 35–40 MINUTES

FRESH
6–8 fresh curry leaves

3 garlic cloves, finely chopped

1-inch piece ginger, peeled and finely shredded

1 onion, finely chopped

1 small green chile, seeded if you like and finely chopped

1 tomato, finely chopped

SPICES
¼ teaspoon ground turmeric

¾ teaspoon cumin seeds

½ teaspoon garam masala

PANTRY
½ cup basmati rice, thoroughly washed

½ cup yellow moong dhal, thoroughly washed

1 teaspoon salt, or to taste

Boiling water, as needed

2 tablespoons oil

2 teaspoons melted ghee, for drizzling (optional)

1. In a large saucepan, mix the rice and dhal (lentils) together and add 2½ cups water. Bring to a boil over high heat, then reduce the heat to medium-low and simmer for 15 minutes. Use a large spoon to lift off any white scum or residue.

2. Add the turmeric and salt and continue to simmer over low heat for a further 10–15 minutes, occasionally stirring and pressing the rice and lentils against the pan with the back of a spoon, until everything is soft and creamy. Add a little boiling water if too thick. Turn off the heat.

3. In a frying pan, heat the oil over medium heat. Add the curry leaves and cumin seeds, then as soon as they start to crackle add the garlic and ginger and stir-fry for 30 seconds.

4. Next, add the onion and fry until soft and golden, then add the garam masala and green chile and fry for 1 minute. Next, add the tomato and fry for 30 seconds.

5. Add the fried mixture to the cooked rice and lentils, then gently stir and cook altogether for a further 5–8 minutes over low heat. Serve with a drizzle of ghee, if you like.

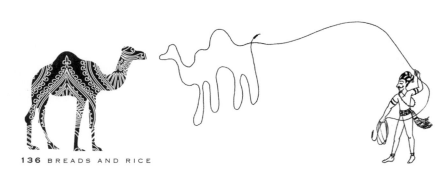

Coconut Rice

For those who like the rich, creamy flavor of coconuts, this dish adds another dimension to enjoying rice. It is full of texture, but can be dry, so serve with sauce-based curries.

SERVES 4 | PREPARATION TIME: 10 MINUTES | COOKING TIME: 5–7 MINUTES

FRESH

8–10 fresh curry leaves

1 cup (3 oz) grated fresh coconut or desiccated coconut

1 recipe cooked Simple Plain Rice (page 134)

SPICES

1 teaspoon mustard seeds

½-inch piece cassia or cinnamon stick

5–6 green cardamom pods, lightly crushed

1 whole dried chile

PANTRY

1 tablespoon coconut oil

Salt, to taste (optional)

2 teaspoons melted ghee (optional)

GARNISH

Crushed mixed seeds and nuts, such as pistachios, almonds, cashews, peanuts, and sesame seeds, gently toasted in a nonstick pan over low heat until golden, let cool, then crushed until coarse with a rolling pin

1. Heat the oil in a frying pan over medium-low heat. Add the mustard seeds, cassia, cardamom, dried chile, and curry leaves and fry gently for 20 seconds.

2. Next, add the coconut and salt and cook for a further 3–4 minutes.

3. Combine the coconut mixture with the Simple Plain Rice, garnish with crushed mixed seeds and nuts, and drizzle with ghee, if you like.

Whole Spice, Crispy Onion, and Lentil Rice

WITH THEIR UNIQUE PEPPERY FLAVOR, PUY LENTILS MAKE THIS RICE DISH
FABULOUS. THE SHAPE OF THE PUY LENTILS HOLDS DURING COOKING AND COMBINES
SUPERBLY WITH THE SPICES. MAKE SURE THE LENTILS ARE COOKED AL DENTE.

SERVES 4 | PREPARATION TIME: 15 MINUTES | COOKING TIME: 20–25 MINUTES

FRESH

½-inch piece ginger, peeled
and finely grated

1 recipe cooked Simple Plain Rice
(page 134)

SPICES

1 black cardamom pod

½ teaspoon grated nutmeg

½-inch cassia or cinnamon stick

2 cloves

½ teaspoon ground turmeric

PANTRY

8 oz Puy lentils (French green
lentils), thoroughly washed

1 scant cup chicken or vegetable stock

½ tablespoon ghee or butter

¼ teaspoon salt (optional)

GARNISH

Crispy Ginger, Onion, and
Garlic (page 238)

4–5 cilantro sprigs, roughly torn

1. In a medium saucepan with a lid, mix the lentils, stock, black cardamom, nutmeg, cassia, cloves, and turmeric together and bring to a boil. Gently stir once, cover with a lid, and reduce the heat to low.

2. Simmer for 20–25 minutes. The lentils should be al dente and not mushy. Once cooked, stir in the grated ginger and ghee and salt, if using, then mix together gently with the Simple Plain Rice.

3. Garnish with Crispy Ginger, Onion, and Garlic and the torn cilantro.

Vegetable Rice

IF YOU ARE LONGING FOR A COMFORTING AND SIMPLE MEAL AT
SUPPERTIME WITH NO FUSS BUT LOTS OF FLAVOR AND GOODNESS,
THEN TRY THIS RICE DISH. FOR EXTRA DEPTH AND TEXTURE DURING
COOKING, ADD A HANDFUL OF COOKED LENTILS OR BEANS.

SERVES 2 AS A MAIN AND 4 AS A SIDE | PREPARATION TIME: 35 MINUTES
COOKING TIME: 15 MINUTES

FRESH

½ onion, finely chopped

2 small green chiles, split
lengthwise down the middle

¼ cauliflower, cut into small
florets and steamed

1 scant cup (4 oz) cooked peas

1 potato, finely
diced and steamed

1 carrot, finely
diced and steamed

2 large tomatoes, seeded
and finely diced

½-inch piece ginger, peeled
and cut into julienne

1 recipe cooked Simple Plain Rice
(page 134), cooked with an Eight Whole
Spice Bouquet Garni (page 248)

1 tablespoon lime juice

2 tablespoons finely
chopped cilantro

SPICES

½ teaspoon cumin seeds

¼ teaspoon ground turmeric

PANTRY

1 tablespoon oil

¼ teaspoon salt, or to taste

1 tablespoon melted ghee, for drizzling

1. Heat the oil in a large frying pan over medium heat. Add
the cumin seeds and, once they start to crackle, add the
onion and green chiles and fry until lightly golden brown.

2. Reduce the heat slightly, add the turmeric and salt, and
fry for 1 minute. Stir in the cooked cauliflower, peas, potato,
and carrot and fry, stirring, for 1–2 minutes.

3. Next, add the tomatoes and ginger and fry for 20 seconds,
then add the cooked rice and lime juice. Stir through gently
and serve with a drizzle of ghee and chopped cilantro.

Tamarind Rice

Tamarind rice is quite possibly the most common and popular accompaniment to South Indian meals, or even baked chicken and fish. The tangy, sweet-spicy, and sticky dressing can be made in advance and used to liven up any leftover rice.

SERVES 4 | PREPARATION TIME: 25 MINUTES | COOKING TIME: 45 MINUTES

FRESH

9–10 fresh curry leaves

1 tablespoon Tamarind Pulp (page 228)

1 small onion, finely chopped

1 recipe cooked Simple Plain Rice (page 134)

SPICES

½ teaspoon fennel seeds

2 dried red chiles

1 teaspoon black mustard seeds

1 teaspoon asafetida

¼ teaspoon ground turmeric

PANTRY

1 tablespoon chana dhal

½ teaspoon light brown sugar

½ teaspoon salt, or to taste

2 tablespoons oil

GARNISH

Crushed mixed seeds and nuts, such as cashews, peanuts, and sesame seeds, gently toasted in a nonstick pan over low heat until golden, let cool, then crushed until coarse with a rolling pin

1. In a nonstick pan over medium-low heat, toast the following until light golden brown: chana dhal, fennel seeds, curry leaves, dried chiles, and mustard seeds, then let cool and grind into a fine powder. Set aside.

2. Mix together the tamarind pulp, sugar, salt, and ½ cup water in a bowl.

3. Heat the oil in a large frying pan over medium-low heat, add the onion, and cook, stirring frequently, until soft and golden. Add the asafetida, turmeric, and spice powder and fry together, while stirring for 30 seconds. Add the tamarind pulp mixture and continue cooking over low heat for 10–12 minutes, or until thick. Stir in the cooked rice, remove from the heat, and garnish with the crushed mixed nuts and seeds.

NOTE: Rice should be cooled once cooked. If you need to make a different quantity of rice, always use 1 measure of dry rice to 2 measures of water.

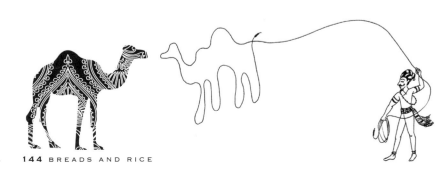

Lemon and Chickpea Rice

THIS FANTASTIC COMBINATION OF RICE AND CHICKPEAS CAN BE ENJOYED
ON ITS OWN OR WITH A CURRY. THE CHICKPEAS ARE HIGHLY NUTRITIOUS
AND PROVIDE A GOOD SOURCE OF PROTEIN IF YOU ARE A VEGETARIAN.

SERVES 4 | PREPARATION TIME: 15 MINUTES | COOKING TIME: 25 MINUTES

FRESH

Zest (cut into fine strips)
and juice of 1½ lemons

2-inch piece ginger, peeled and
cut into julienne

3 tablespoons finely
chopped cilantro

SPICES

1 tablespoon mustard seeds

1 tablespoon cumin seeds

1 dried red chile

¼ teaspoon ground turmeric

PANTRY

1 cup basmati rice, thoroughly washed

2 cups boiling water

1 teaspoon salt, or to taste

2 tablespoons oil

1 cup cooked chickpeas

OPTIONAL GARNISH

Curry Leaves, Garlic, Ginger,
and Red Chile (page 240)

¼ cup roasted peanuts,
lightly crushed (see Note)

1. Pour the rice into the boiling water, together with
½ teaspoon salt and zest of ½ lemon. Cook for 10 minutes,
then drain.

2. Heat the oil in a small frying pan over medium heat.
Add the mustard and cumin seeds and as they begin to
pop, turn the heat down.

3. Add the ginger and dried red chile and fry for
30 seconds. Then add the chickpeas together with the
turmeric, the remaining lemon zest and remaining salt
and cook for 1 minute. Transfer to a serving bowl.

4. Add the drained rice to the bowl and stir in the
chopped cilantro and lemon juice. Garnish with Curry
Leaves, Garlic, Ginger, and Red Chile and crushed roasted
peanuts, if you like.

NOTE: Store-bought roasted peanuts work well.

Crab Fried Rice

INSPIRED BY SOUTH INDIAN FLAVORS, THIS SWEET, SOUR, AND ZESTY
RICE DISH IS A DREAM FOR EVERY SEAFOOD LOVER. MAKE SURE THE RICE
HAS COMPLETELY COOLED DOWN BEFORE USING HERE, OR,
ALTERNATIVELY HAS BEEN MADE EARLIER AND KEPT IN THE FRIDGE.

SERVES 2 AS A MAIN AND 4 AS A SIDE DISH | PREPARATION TIME: 20 MINUTES
COOKING TIME: 15 MINUTES

FRESH

1 tablespoon Tamarind Pulp (page 228)

8–10 fresh curry leaves

½ onion, finely chopped

1 celery rib, finely chopped

3 garlic cloves, finely chopped

½-inch piece ginger, peeled and finely shredded

3 red chiles, seeded, if you like, and finely sliced

5 oz crabmeat

2 tablespoons finely chopped cilantro

Juice of ½ lemon or lime

1 recipe cooked Simple Plain Rice (page 134), preferably cooked the night before

SPICES

3 teaspoons fennel seeds

2 teaspoons black mustard seeds

1 teaspoon cumin seeds

2 teaspoons garam masala

1 teaspoon ground turmeric

PANTRY

1 tablespoon coconut milk powder

¼ teaspoon granulated sugar

1 teaspoon salt, or to taste

3–4 tablespoons oil

GARNISH

4 green onions, sliced

4–5 cilantro sprigs

Melted ghee or sour cream

1. Mix the tamarind pulp, coconut milk powder, sugar, and salt together, then set aside.

2. Heat the oil in a large frying pan over medium-low heat. Add the fennel, mustard, and cumin seeds and fry for 20–30 seconds, then add the curry leaves.

3. Add the onion and celery and fry for 2 minutes, or until lightly golden. Next, add the garlic, ginger, and chiles and fry over medium heat for 1 minute.

4. Add the garam masala and turmeric and fry for 1 minute. Reduce the heat, pour in the tamarind mixture and gently simmer for 2–3 minutes.

5. Stir in the crabmeat and the chopped cilantro sprigs, lemon or lime juice, and cooked rice and fry until the rice is fluffy and toasted.

6. Garnish with sliced green onions, cilantro and a drizzle of ghee, if you like. Serve immediately.

Saffron and Cashew Nut Rice

This fragrant rice goes particularly well with meat and fish dishes and is traditionally served as part of Indian festival meals. The subtle taste of saffron and the crunchy cashew nuts make it a lovely treat at a dinner party or any special occasion.

SERVES 4 | PREPARATION TIME: 10 MINUTES | COOKING TIME: 20 MINUTES

SPICES

1-inch cassia or cinnamon stick

1 star anise

2–3 cloves

6–8 small green cardamom pods, slightly crushed

2–3 saffron threads soaked in 1 teaspoon milk (see Saffron Essence, page 228)

PANTRY

2 tablespoons ghee or oil

2 tablespoons cashew nuts, soaked in a pinch of ground turmeric and hot water

1 cup basmati rice, thoroughly washed

2 cups hot water

½ teaspoon salt, or to taste

1. Heat 1 tablespoon ghee in a heavy pan with a tight-fitting lid over medium-low heat. Add the drained cashew nuts and gently fry for 20 seconds.

2. Add the cassia, star anise, cloves, and cardamom pods and continue to fry for 30 seconds.

3. Add the rice, stir gently to coat, then add the hot water, salt, and saffron threads, including the soaking milk, and bring to a boil. Gently stir once, cover, and reduce the heat to low.

4. Simmer for about 18 minutes. Keep the lid on and remove the pan from the heat. Leave to stand, covered, for a further 5 minutes. Fluff up with a fork and gently stir in the remaining ghee.

NOTE: If you need to make a different quantity of rice, always use 1 measure of dry rice to 2 measures of water.

Chicken Pulao

WONDERFUL, SIMPLE, AND SATISFYING, CHICKEN PULAO NEVER FAILS TO
IMPRESS AT A CASUAL LUNCH WITH FRIENDS OR A FAMILY DINNER. UNLIKE
A BIRYANI WHERE THE MEAT AND RICE ARE COOKED SEPARATELY, A PULAO DISH
HAS THE RICE AND MEAT OR VEGETABLES COOKED TOGETHER IN ONE POT.

SERVES 4 | PREPARATION TIME: 35 MINUTES | COOKING TIME: 1 HOUR

FRESH

6 garlic cloves

1-inch piece ginger, peeled

2 tablespoons plain yogurt

½ large onion, finely sliced

2 lb skinless chicken on the bone,
cut into medium pieces

2 tablespoons finely
chopped cilantro

SPICES

6 cloves

2-inch cassia or cinnamon stick

4 bay leaves

2 black cardamom pods

6–8 green cardamom pods

1 tablespoon garam masala

1 teaspoon ground cumin,
plus extra for sprinkling

1 teaspoon paprika

1 teaspoon chile powder

1 teaspoon ground turmeric

PANTRY

1¾ cup vegetable or chicken
stock or water

2 teaspoons salt, or to taste

3 tablespoons oil

1 cup basmati rice, thoroughly washed

SERVE

1 lime, cut into wedges

1. Using a mortar and pestle, make a fine paste with the garlic and ginger. Set aside.

2. In a small bowl, mix together the yogurt, stock or water, and 1 teaspoon salt. Set aside.

3. Heat the oil in a large, heavy pan over low heat. Add the whole cassia, bay leaves, and cardamom pods and fry for 20 seconds, then add the onion and fry for 20 minutes, or until golden brown. Turn up the heat, then add the garlic and ginger paste and fry for 1–2 minutes.

4. Add the chicken and ground garam masala, cumin, paprika, chile powder, and turmeric and mix together well. Cover and cook for 8–10 minutes, stirring occasionally.

5. Add half the yogurt mixture, stir through, bring to a boil, cover, and cook for a further 10 minutes, stirring occasionally.

6. Now add the rice, cilantro, 1 teaspoon salt, and the remaining yogurt mixture. Bring to a boil, then reduce the heat, cover, and cook for 16–18 minutes, or until the rice liquid has evaporated and the chicken and rice are tender. Remove from the heat and let rest for 5–7 minutes with the lid on. Sprinkle with ground cumin and serve immediately with lime wedges.

NOTE: Chicken on the bone releases a more intense flavor to the dish.

Lamb Biryani

THIS IS A COMPLETE, "BOWL ONLY"–STYLE SUPPER. MAKING BIRYANI
IS TIME-CONSUMING, BUT THE END RESULT—THE TEXTURE AND WONDERFUL
FLAVORS AND AROMAS—MAKE IT WELL WORTH IT. ALTERNATIVELY,
PREPARE THE FRAGRANT LAMB MASALA THE DAY BEFORE AND
LAYER WITH THE COOKED RICE ONCE THE RICE IS READY TO SERVE.

SERVES 4–5 | PREPARATION TIME: 3–4 HOURS | COOKING TIME: 1 HOUR

FRESH

1½ onions

6 garlic cloves

1½-inch piece ginger

2 green chiles

2 lb boneless lamb, cut into cubes

1 recipe Simple Plain Rice (page 134)

SPICES

4 green cardamom pods, slightly cracked

2 black cardamom pods, slightly cracked

6 cloves

4 bay leaves

1½ teaspoons cumin seeds

1½-inch cassia or cinnamon stick

2½ teaspoons garam masala

Large pinch of saffron threads, soaked in ¼ cup warm milk (see Saffron Essence, page 228)

PANTRY

¼ can (4 oz) diced tomatoes

1 tablespoon desiccated coconut

3 tablespoons ghee or oil

2 teaspoons salt, or to taste

GARNISH

Crispy Ginger, Onion, and Garlic (page 238)

1 teaspoon melted ghee

1. Blitz together the onions, garlic, ginger, chiles, diced tomatoes, and coconut in a high-speed blender until it is a smooth paste.

2. In a large pan with a lid, heat the ghee over medium-low heat, then add the whole cardamom pods, cloves, bay leaves, cumin, and cassia and fry for 20 seconds, or until golden.

3. Add the lamb and tomato and coconut paste, stir until everything is coated, then cover with the lid and cook for 25 minutes over low heat. Uncover and cook for a further 20 minutes, stirring frequently.

4. Once the oil has separated, the sauce has thickened, and the lamb is cooked and tender, add the garam masala and salt. Stir and cook for 2 minutes, then turn off the heat.

5. Once the Simple Plain Rice is ready, immediately assemble the biryani. Spread a large spoonful of rice over the base of a pan with a lid. Next, spread a layer of cooked lamb and alternate with the rice and lamb until you finish with a layer of rice.

6. Last, drizzle the saffron milk all over the layered biryani, cover, and seal with foil. Place the lid on top and cook over a very low heat for 10 minutes. Garnish with Crispy Ginger, Onion, and Garlic and a drizzle of ghee.

NOTE: If making the lamb masala ahead of time, reduce the cooking time by 1 minute and reheat thoroughly before layering with the fresh-cooked rice.

SIX
Potatoes

1 SPICY SWEET-POTATO WEDGES

PREHEAT the oven to 350°F.

CUT 2 large unpeeled sweet potatoes into wedges and place on a heavy baking sheet.

CRUSH 1 teaspoon fennel seeds, 1 teaspoon cumin seeds, ½–1 teaspoon red pepper flakes, and 1 teaspoon salt, or to taste, using a mortar and pestle.

MIX with 2 tablespoons oil. Scatter in 3 garlic cloves, lightly crushed with skins on, and toss everything together.

ROAST for 30–45 minutes, turning once.

2 MUMBAI ALOO

HEAT 3 tablespoons oil in a pan over medium heat.

ADD 1 teaspoon cumin seeds and 1 teaspoon mustard seeds. After 3–4 seconds add 3 cups (1 lb) diced cooked potato and ½-inch piece ginger, peeled and grated, ½ teaspoon ground turmeric, 1 teaspoon ground coriander, ½ teaspoon red pepper flakes, ½ teaspoon dried mango powder, and ½ teaspoon salt.

GENTLY keep tossing together and at the same time crushing the odd potato with the back of a spoon for 6–8 minutes.

GARNISH with 2 tablespoons finely chopped cilantro and a large pinch of chaat masala.

3 POTATO, PEAS, AND TOMATO

HEAT 2 tablespoons oil in a pan over low heat.

ADD 1 bay leaf, 1 teaspoon cumin seeds, 2 finely chopped garlic cloves, and ½-inch piece ginger, peeled and grated.

MIX 2 tablespoons Caramelized Onion Paste (page 231), 1 tablespoon tamarind extract, and 2 tablespoons tomato purée; pour mixture into pan.

FRY for 2 minutes, add 1 teaspoon ground turmeric, 1 teaspoon garam masala, 1 teaspoon ground coriander, and 1½ teaspoons salt.

STIR and cook for 1 minute.

ADD 1 scant cup (4 oz) frozen peas and fry for 1 minute, then add 1½ cups (8 oz) diced cooked potato and cook, stirring constantly, 3–4 minutes.

REMOVE from the heat and stir in 2 finely chopped fresh tomatoes.

4 CRUSHED POTATOES

PLACE 1 lb peeled and chopped potatoes, with a Three Whole Spice Bouquet Garni (page 248) and 2 teaspoons salt in a large pan of water.

BOIL 8–10 minutes until cooked through. Drain and reserve.

HEAT 1 tablespoon oil or ghee in the pan, add ½ teaspoon cumin seeds, and gently fry for 20 seconds.

ADD ½ leek (2 oz), finely chopped, and 1½ garlic cloves, finely chopped, and fry for 30 seconds over low heat until caramelized.

POUR in 2 tablespoons coconut milk. Add the potatoes and mix and mash everything together. Drizzle with ghee or butter.

GARNISH with finely chopped cilantro.

5 STUFFED POTATO AND PEA CAKES

PULSE ½ cup (3 oz) peas, ¼ cups (1 oz) paneer, 1 teaspoon grated ginger, ½ green chile, ¼ teaspoon dried mango powder, ¼ teaspoon garam masala, ¼ teaspoon salt, and 1 tablespoon cilantro in a high-speed blender.

MIX together 2 cups (1 lb) mashed potatoes, 1 teaspoon ground cumin, 1 teaspoon ground coriander, 1 teaspoon ground fennel, a large pinch of chile powder, ¼ teaspoon ground ginger, ½ teaspoon chaat masala, 1 teaspoon salt, and 2 tablespoons cornstarch.

OIL your hands, take a heaping tablespoonful of the potato mixture, and place in the palm of your hand. Flatten and place 2 teaspoonfuls of the paneer and pea mixture in the middle. Fold in all the sides and roll into a ball then flatten slightly. Repeat.

HEAT 6 tablespoons oil in a frying pan. Fry 2–3 cakes at a time on both sides 2–3 minutes, or until golden.

6 FIVE-SPICE POTATO SALAD

HEAT ¼ cup oil in a heavy pan over medium heat.

ADD 1 teaspoon panch phoran, then after about a minute of stirring add 1 lb halved baby potatoes. Next, add 1 teaspoon ground turmeric, 1½ teaspoons garam masala or ground cinnamon, 1 teaspoon red pepper flakes, and sea salt, to taste.

FRY and keep stirring for 2 minutes. Pour in 2 tablespoons water, cover, and simmer over low heat for 8–10 minutes. Remove the lid, turn up the heat and cook, stirring, until the water has completely evaporated and the potatoes are cooked through and starting to sizzle and fry.

REMOVE from the heat and gently stir in 2 finely chopped tomatoes, 1 tablespoon finely chopped fresh mint and 1 tablespoon finely chopped cilantro.

salads

CHAPTER 5

Shredded Raw Veg Salad with Spice Dressing and Nuts

THIS SALAD COMPRISES DELICATE STRIPS OF FRESH VEGETABLES,
BOLDLY TEMPERED WITH MUSTARD SEEDS, GINGER, CHILE, AND LEMON.

SERVES 2 AS A MAIN OR 4 AS A SIDE | PREPARATION TIME: 20 MINUTES
COOKING TIME: 5 MINUTES

FRESH
1 bunch radishes, finely sliced

2 carrots, thinly sliced

2 zucchini, cut into thin
slices or ribbons

¼ daikon, cut into thin
slices or ribbons

3 green onions, finely shredded

4–5 fresh curry leaves

Juice of ¼ lemon

¼-inch piece ginger, peeled
and finely grated

SPICES
¼ teaspoon yellow, brown, or black
mustard seeds

Large pinch of red pepper flakes

PANTRY
1 tablespoon olive oil

Salt, or to taste

OPTIONAL GARNISH
1 tablespoon Mixed Nuts and Seeds
(page 240), lightly crushed

5 cilantro sprigs, cut in half

1. Place the radishes, carrots, zucchini, daikon, and green onions in a large bowl.

2. Heat the oil in a small frying pan over low heat. Add the mustard seeds and curry leaves and fry for 20 seconds. Add to the bowl of vegetables.

3. Then squeeze in the lemon juice and sprinkle in the red pepper flakes, ginger, and salt. Gently toss together.

4. Garnish with crushed mixed nuts and seeds, finishing off with a scattering of cilantro sprigs.

Kale, Chickpea, Mint, and Preserved Lemon Salad

A REFRESHING AND HEALTHY SALAD MADE SUBSTANTIAL BY THE ADDITION OF CHICKPEAS. IT IS ALSO SUITABLE AS A SIDE DISH, OR ENJOY ON ITS OWN WITH BARBECUED SLICES OF PANEER OR HALLOUMI CHEESE.

SERVES 2 AS A MAIN OR 4 AS A SIDE | PREPARATION TIME: 20–25 MINUTES

FRESH

1 garlic clove, finely crushed

½ teaspoon finely shredded mint leaves

2 teaspoons lemon juice

1 cup cooked chickpeas, lightly crushed with the back of a fork

5 oz kale, finely shredded

1 tablespoon preserved lemon, finely sliced

SPICES

¼ teaspoon cumin seeds and ¼ teaspoon fennel seeds, lightly toasted and crushed

¼ teaspoon red pepper flakes (optional)

PANTRY

1 tablespoon oil

Salt, to taste

1. Whisk together the oil, crushed cumin and fennel seeds, red pepper flakes, if using, garlic, mint, lemon juice, and salt.

2. Place the chickpeas and kale in a large bowl.

3. Pour the dressing over and scatter with the preserved lemon.

Tomato and Pickled Ginger Salad

This is a juicy and effortless tomato salad, which works really well with Japanese pickled ginger and the sticky, sweet-sour chaat masala and balsamic dressing.

SERVES 4 AS A SIDE | PREPARATION TIME: 20 MINUTES

FRESH
8 tomatoes, sliced, or cut into quarters
3 teaspoons Japanese pickled ginger, finely shredded

SPICES
1 teaspoon chaat masala
¼ teaspoon red pepper flakes

PANTRY
1½ tablespoons oil
3 teaspoons balsamic vinegar
Salt, to taste

OPTIONAL GARNISH
2 teaspoons finely torn cilantro leaves
¼ teaspoon nigella seeds

1. Combine the tomatoes and pickled ginger in a large bowl.

2. Whisk together the oil, vinegar, chaat masala, red pepper flakes, and salt.

3. Pour the dressing over the tomatoes, then, using your hands, toss and coat very gently.

4. Garnish with cilantro and nigella seeds, if you like.

Avocado, Corn, Chile, and Cilantro Salad

SERVE WITH FINELY SLICED GRIDDLED BREAD AND ENJOY AS A PROPER MEAL
OR SERVE ALONGSIDE BROILED FISH, GRILLED MEATS, AND PASTRIES.

SERVES 2 AS A MAIN OR 4 AS A SIDE | PREPARATION TIME: 20 MINUTES
COOKING TIME: 30 MINUTES

FRESH
2–3 whole ears corn
½ lime, cut into wedges
3 firm, ripe avocados, finely sliced or cubed
½ red onion, finely sliced
1 tablespoon roughly chopped cilantro
½ large red chile, seeded if you like and finely chopped
1 garlic clove, minced

SPICES
¼ teaspoon toasted cumin seeds, lightly crushed, plus a pinch for garnish

PANTRY
1 tablespoon melted butter
Salt and black pepper, to taste
1 tablespoon oil
2 teaspoons balsamic vinegar

1. Steam the corn ears for 15–17 minutes.

2. Preheat the broiler. Brush the corn ears with the melted butter and place under the hot broiler. Cook, turning frequently, until lightly toasted.

3. Rub the corn all over with lime wedges, then cut away the kernels by slicing down the sides of the ears with a sharp knife.

4. Place the avocados, corn kernels (reserving a little for the garnish), onion, cilantro, and chile into a large bowl and season with salt and pepper.

5. Whisk together the oil, vinegar, garlic, and crushed cumin and pour over the corn salad. Mix well until everything is coated with the dressing.

6. Garnish with the reserved corn kernels and toasted cumin, if you like.

Bean and Lentil Salad with Garlic and Ginger

This healthy and nourishing mixture of mung beans, lentils, and chickpeas is fried together with strips of garlic until crispy and nutty and finished off with carrot, ginger, and sliced red onion. You can find the sprouted legumes ready-packed in most supermarkets or health-food stores. This salad can be served warm.

SERVES 2 AS MAIN DISH OR 4 AS A SIDE | PREPARATION TIME: 15 MINUTES
COOKING TIME: 15 MINUTES

FRESH

3 garlic cloves, very finely sliced

4 cups (14 oz) mixed sprouted beans and lentils

2 large carrots, sliced into fine ribbons

4–5 chicory leaves, such as endive or radicchio (optional)

¼ red onion, finely sliced

5–6 cilantro sprigs, cut in half

¼-inch piece ginger, peeled and finely shredded

SPICES

¼ teaspoon ground coriander

¼ teaspoon ground cumin

½ teaspoon red pepper flakes

PANTRY

2 tablespoons oil, plus extra for drizzling (optional)

Salt, to taste

1. Heat the oil in a large frying pan over low heat. Add the garlic and fry for 20 seconds.

2. Stir in the sprouted beans, together with the ground coriander, ground cumin, pepper flakes, and salt. Keep tossing and frying for 6–7 minutes, or until crispy and nutty to taste. Turn off the heat and cool.

3. Place the carrots, chicory leaves, if using, onion, cilantro, and ginger in a bowl, then add the toasted sprouted beans and lentils and mix together well. Drizzle with oil, if using, and serve.

pickles and chutneys

CHAPTER 6

Cilantro and Peanut Chutney

VIBRANT AND ZESTY, THIS GREEN CHUTNEY TAKES JUST MINUTES TO MAKE,
ESPECIALLY IF USING STORE-BOUGHT ROASTED PEANUTS. SERVE
WITH SESAME AND GINGER CHICKEN SKEWERS (PAGE 40) OR STEAK
AND OTHER COOKED MEATS, NAAN BREADS (PAGE 127), AND RICE.

SERVES 4 | PREPARATION TIME: 15 MINUTES

FRESH

5 oz cilantro, roughly chopped
(including stalks)

1 small green chile

4 tablespoons lemon juice

PANTRY

⅓ cup dry-roasted peanuts (see Note),
finely crushed with a mortar and
pestle or with a rolling pin

3 teaspoons light brown sugar

½ teaspoon salt, or to taste

Combine the cilantro, chile, peanuts, sugar, salt, lemon juice, and 1 tablespoon water in a small blender and blitz until smooth.

NOTE: Store-bought peanuts work perfectly well.

Green Mango, Apple, Cilantro, and Mint Relish

THIS IS A TERRIFIC COMBINATION OF INGREDIENTS THAT
RESULTS IN A REFRESHING AND PERKY MIX OF SWEET,
SOUR, AND SPICY. THIS RELISH IS MOSTLY EATEN WITH FRITTERS,
PASTIES, AND PANEER-BASED SNACKS.

SERVES 4 | PREPARATION TIME: 20 MINUTES

FRESH

1 small green mango, pitted
and roughly chopped

½ green apple, peeled, cored,
and roughly chopped

¼ red onion, roughly chopped

1 green onion, roughly chopped

1 bunch (2 oz) cilantro, roughly chopped

1 bunch (2 oz) mint, roughly chopped

1 small green chile, roughly chopped

SPICES

½ teaspoon pomegranate seed powder

1 teaspoon chaat masala

PANTRY

¼ teaspoon light brown sugar

¼ teaspoon salt, or to taste

Combine all the ingredients in a blender
and blitz until combined, but still coarse.

Tomato, Date, and Tamarind Relish

THIS IS A FRESH, CLEAN-TASTING RELISH THAT HAS A REMARKABLE FRUITY, SOUR, AND CHILE EDGE. FOR BEST RESULTS, USE GOOD-QUALITY TOMATOES AND SERVE WITH GRILLED MEATS, PANEER, SAVORY FRITTERS, AND PASTIES.

SERVES 4 | PREPARATION TIME: 15 MINUTES

FRESH

2 medium tomatoes (about 8 oz), peeled and seeded

1 small green chile

1 garlic clove

½-inch piece ginger, peeled and grated

1 tablespoon finely chopped cilantro

6 tablespoons Tamarind Pulp (page 228)

SPICES

½ teaspoon toasted cumin seeds

½ teaspoon ground coriander

PANTRY

4 oz pitted dried dates, soaked in 2 cups hot water until soft and plump

¼ teaspoon salt, or to taste

1. Heat a frying pan over medium heat and toast the cumin seeds, gently tossing for 30 seconds, or until dark brown. Remove immediately and crush using a mortar and pestle or rolling pin.

2. Add all the ingredients to a small blender, including the date soaking water, and pulse gently until roughly blended.

3. Place in a clean screw-top jar and refrigerate for up to 3 days.

NOTE: This relish freezes very well.

Garlic and Red Chile Chutney

NOT ONLY CAN YOU ENJOY THIS AS A CHUTNEY, BUT ALSO AS A PASTE
IN COOKING—ADD TO SOUPS, MARINADES, AND OTHER SAUCE-BASED DISHES
TO BRING THEM ALIVE. THIS IS USUALLY EATEN IN SMALL QUANTITIES,
BUT IF RAW GARLIC IS TOO STRONG AND NOT TO YOUR TASTE, ROAST THE
GARLIC CLOVES FIRST, THEN BLEND WITH THE REST OF THE INGREDIENTS.

MAKES 4–6 TABLESPOONS | PREPARATION TIME: 10 MINUTES

FRESH
1 whole garlic head, peeled and
finely chopped or crushed
2–3 teaspoons lemon juice

SPICES
3 teaspoons chile powder, preferably
Kashmiri chile powder

PANTRY
3–4 tablespoons oil
½ teaspoon salt, or to taste

Combine the garlic, lemon juice, and chile
powder in a blender with half the oil and the
salt and blitz, then add the remaining oil and
continue to blend until smooth.

HOW TO MAKE
Yogurt

Yogurt has so many uses—it makes an excellent base for marinades, dips, and toppings and is often used to add richness and a tang to sauces during cooking. If this is your first time making yogurt, start by checking it after 4 hours and stop when it reaches a flavor and consistency you like. Avoid stirring the yogurt until it has fully set. The exact time will depend on the cultures used, the temperature of the yogurt, and your yogurt preferences—the longer yogurt sits, the thicker and more tart it becomes.

MAKES ABOUT 4 LB YOGURT | PREPARATION TIME: ABOUT 6 HOURS
COOKING TIME: 15 MINUTES | SETTING TIME: 4–8 HOURS

EQUIPMENT

HEAVY PAN WITH A LID
WOODEN SPOON
THERMOMETER
SMALL MEASURING CUP OR BOWL
WHISK

heat

cool

whisk

1

Preheat the oven to 325°F. Pour 10 cups whole milk into a heavy pan with a lid and heat over medium-high heat. Warm the milk to just below boiling, about 200°F. Gently stir the milk, making sure the bottom doesn't scorch and the milk doesn't boil over.

note For best results use organic whole milk.

2

Let the milk cool until it is just warm to the touch, 110°–115°F. Stir occasionally to prevent a skin from forming.

3

Scoop out about 1 cup of warm milk and add it to ½ cup plain whole-milk yogurt (containing active cultures) in a bowl. Whisk until the yogurt is dissolved into the milk and the mixture is smooth.

5

Cover the mixture with the lid and wrap the pan with kitchen towels. Place in the turned-off oven. Let the yogurt set for at least 4 hours, or overnight.

4 hours

pour

4

While whisking the warm milk gently, pour the yogurt mixture into the milk pan. Switch off the oven at this point.

6

Once the yogurt has set to your liking, remove it from the oven. If you see any watery whey on the surface of the yogurt, you can either drain it off or whisk it back into the yogurt before transferring it to a container. Whisking also gives the yogurt a more consistent creamy texture. Transfer into a sterilized jar, seal with a tight-fitting sterilized lid, and refrigerate for up to 2 weeks.

Cucumber, Carrot, and Mint Chutney

THIS IS A CLASSIC YOGURT CHUTNEY. THIS RECIPE HAS TAKEN THIS CHUTNEY ONE STEP FURTHER BY ADDING CARROT, WHICH GIVES IT AN EXTRA BITE. IT'S A COOLING ACCOMPANIMENT TO ANY FIERY CURRY.

SERVES 4 | PREPARATION TIME: 15 MINUTES

FRESH

5 oz carrots (2 medium), grated

5 oz cucumber (⅔ medium), grated and squeezed dry with a cloth

¼ garlic clove, minced

1 cup (8 oz) Greek yogurt

¼ small green chile, seeded if you like and finely chopped

SPICES

¼ teaspoon toasted cumin seeds, lightly crushed, reserving a pinch for a garnish

Black salt or table salt, to taste

Large pinch of chaat masala

PANTRY

¼ teaspoon dried mint

OPTIONAL GARNISH

1 tablespoon finely chopped Green Onion, Cilantro, and Mint (see page 232)

Combine all the ingredients (except the garnish) in a bowl and mix together. Garnish, if you like, and serve cold.

South Indian Eggplant Pickle

EGGPLANTS ARE A POPULAR VEGETABLE IN INDIAN COOKING, AND ARE USED IN MANY INNOVATIVE WAYS. THIS TANGY, SWEET PICKLE HAS A FIERY KICK AND PARTNERS WELL WITH PANCAKES, RICE, DHAL DISHES, AND CRISPY CRACKERS.

MAKES 1½ CUPS | PREPARATION TIME: 2 HOURS | DRAINING TIME: 3 HOURS

FRESH

1 lb eggplant, diced into medium-sized cubes

4-inch piece ginger, peeled

4 garlic cloves

8–9 fresh curry leaves

3½ teaspoons Tamarind Pulp (page 228)

SPICES

1 tablespoon black mustard seeds

3½ teaspoons fennel seeds

1 tablespoon cumin seeds

3 teaspoons ground turmeric

2½ teaspoons chile powder

PANTRY

1½ tablespoons salt

½ cup pickling vinegar

1 cup light brown sugar

½ cup mustard seed oil or vegetable oil

1. Place the eggplant in a large colander, coat and gently massage with the salt, then let drain for about 3 hours.

2. Take handfuls of eggplant and squeeze out the water until very dry.

3. Use a mortar and pestle or a small blender to grind the ginger, garlic, and 1 tablespoon of the vinegar until a fine paste forms. Set aside.

4. Heat the oil in a large, heavy frying pan over medium heat. (If using mustard seed oil, see page 15.) Fry the eggplant cubes in 2 batches for 3–4 minutes, or until soft and golden, removing each batch with a slotted spoon and setting aside.

5. Reduce the heat, and in the same pan, gently fry the mustard, fennel, and cumin seeds and the curry leaves for 20 seconds.

6. Add the ginger and garlic paste and fry for 2–3 minutes, then add the turmeric and chile powder and fry for 30 seconds.

7. Pour in the remaining vinegar, tamarind pulp, and sugar, stir through, and cook for 1 minute, then add the eggplant cubes and stir-fry for a further 12–15 minutes, or until the liquid has reduced and it has become sticky.

8. Remove the pan from the heat and let cool completely. Place in a sterilized jar with a tight-fitting lid, seal, and store in the refrigerator for up to 6 weeks.

Fruit Chutney

THIS CHUTNEY IS SOFT, GOOEY, AND EDGY, SO IT'S WELL SUITED
TO HOT CURRIES AND BREADS, BUT CHEEKILY SITS WELL IN
CHEESE SANDWICHES OR AS PART OF A CHEESE BOARD.

SERVES 4 | PREPARATION TIME: 30 MINUTES | COOKING TIME: 20 MINUTES

FRESH

⅓ cup (2 oz) finely chopped apples

⅓ cup (2 oz) finely chopped pears

3 tablespoons Tamarind Pulp (page 228)

1 garlic clove, crushed

½ teaspoon grated ginger

SPICES

2 teaspoons chile powder

1 teaspoon toasted cumin seeds

½ teaspoon ground turmeric

½ teaspoon black salt or chaat masala

PANTRY

1 cup raisins

⅓ cup dried pitted dates, finely chopped

¾ cup cider vinegar

3 tablespoons light brown sugar

Salt, to taste

1. Combine all the ingredients, plus ¼ cup water, in a heavy pan over medium-low heat and stir constantly until the sugar has dissolved.

2. Reduce the heat to low and simmer gently, stirring frequently and periodically checking if any extra water is needed, for about 20 minutes or until the fruit is soft.

3. Remove the pan from the heat and let cool completely. Place in a sterilized jar with a tight-fitting lid, seal, and store in the refrigerator for up to 6 weeks.

Apple Pickle

MAKE THIS PICKLE IN ADVANCE, AS THE SPICES NEED TO INFUSE
AND SETTLE. THE TOASTED SPICES MAKE A REAL DIFFERENCE
TO THIS TART APPLE CONDIMENT. EAT ALONGSIDE CHEESE AND
PLAIN PARANTHA (SEE NOTE PAGE 120) OR OTHER BREADS.

SERVES 4–6 | PREPARATION TIME: 30 MINUTES | STANDING TIME: 1½ HOURS

FRESH

8 oz sour cooking apples, cored and thinly sliced

1 red chile, slit lengthwise down the middle

6–8 whole garlic cloves

7–8 fresh curry leaves

SPICES

2 teaspoons mustard seeds

1 teaspoon fennel seeds

1 tablespoon chile powder

½ teaspoon ground turmeric

½ teaspoon fenugreek seeds

PANTRY

3 teaspoons light brown sugar

2 teaspoons salt, or to taste

2–3 tablespoons oil

¼ cup white wine vinegar

1. Heat a nonstick pan over low heat. Add the mustard and fennel seeds and toast and toss for 40–60 seconds. Let cool and grind to a powder using a mortar and pestle. Set aside.

2. In a large bowl, mix together the apples, chile powder, turmeric, sugar, and salt, making sure the apples are well coated. Leave to stand for 10 minutes.

3. Heat the oil in a heavy pan or wok over medium-low heat. Add the red chile, garlic, curry leaves, and fenugreek seeds and fry gently for 30–40 seconds.

4. Stir in the mustard and fennel powder and keep mixing and frying for 1 minute.

5. Stir in the apples and vinegar, making sure the apples are all well coated, and cook for a further 5 minutes.

6. Remove the pan from the heat, cover, and let stand for 1–1½ hours. Once cooled completely, place in a sterilized jar with a tight-fitting lid, seal, and store in the refrigerator for up to 5 weeks.

Garlic, Ginger, and Red Chile Pickle

WHEN THESE THREE BOLD FLAVORS COME TOGETHER, THEY HAVE THE
POWER TO TRANSFORM ANY DHAL, PARANTHA, OR VEGETABLE DISH. THE LONGER
IT STEWS IN SPICES, THE MORE TENDER AND SWEET THIS PICKLE BECOMES.

SERVES 4 | PREPARATION TIME: 15 MINUTES | COOKING TIME: 15–18 MINUTES

FRESH

18 garlic cloves (1–2 heads), cut into thick slices

4-inch piece ginger, peeled and cut into julienne

2–4 whole bird's eye red chiles

SPICES

¾ teaspoon fenugreek seeds

½ teaspoon ground turmeric

¼ teaspoon chile powder

PANTRY

1½ tablespoons oil

⅔ cup pickling vinegar

1 teaspoon light brown sugar

¼ teaspoon salt, or to taste

1. Heat the oil in a frying pan over medium-low heat.

2. Add the fenugreek seeds and fry for 20 seconds, then add the garlic followed by the ginger and stir-fry for 4–5 minutes.

3. Add the turmeric, chile powder, vinegar, whole chiles, sugar, and salt. Reduce the heat and cook, stirring, for 10–12 minutes, or until the liquid has evaporated and the garlic is tender. Use at once or transfer to a sterilized jar with a tight-fitting lid, seal, and store in the refrigerator for up to 2 weeks.

Sticky, Hot Mango and Lime Pickle

EVERYTHING A PICKLE SHOULD BE—STICKY, HOT, AND ESSENTIAL.
A RESTAURANT FAVORITE, IT IS EATEN IN ABUNDANCE WITH
POPPADUMS AND FRIED SNACKS.

MAKES ABOUT 3 OZ | PREPARATION TIME: 10 MINUTES
STANDING TIME: 15 MINUTES | COOKING TIME: 10–15 MINUTES

FRESH

4 mangoes, peeled and cut
into medium-sized cubes

Zest and juice of 1 lime

SPICES

2 tablespoons chile powder

2 teaspoons panch phoran (page 13)

PANTRY

1¾ teaspoons salt

¾ cup (6 oz) light brown sugar

2 tablespoons oil

1. In a bowl, toss the mangoes with 1½ teaspoons salt and the chile powder. Leave to stand for 15 minutes.

2. Heat the oil in a large frying pan or wok over medium-low heat. Add the panch phoran and stir-fry for 25 seconds.

3. Next, add the chile-coated mango cubes, toss and cook for 6–8 minutes, then add the lime zest, juice, and salt to taste. Cover and cook for 5–7 minutes.

4. Add the sugar and ¼ teaspoon salt and cook, uncovered, until any liquid has evaporated and the mangoes are tender but not mushy.

5. Remove the pan from the heat and let cool. Place in a sterilized jar with a tight-fitting lid, seal, and store in the refrigerator for up to 3 weeks.

Preserved Lemons and Peppercorns with Ginger and Garlic

GIVEN TIME, THIS HEALTHY AYURVEDIC PICKLE JUST KEEPS ON GETTING BETTER, AS THE RIND BECOMES MORE TENDER AND ROBUST. FINELY CHOP THIS PICKLE AND USE IN SALADS OR AS PART OF MARINADES, DRESSINGS, AND GARNISHES. OTHERWISE, EAT JUST SIMPLY AS AN ACCOMPANIMENT TO MAIN MEALS AND SNACKS.

MAKES ABOUT 8 OZ | PREPARATION TIME: 15 MINUTES

FRESH

6–7 lemons, halved then each half cut into 3 wedges

8–10 whole garlic cloves, patted dry

4-inch piece ginger, peeled, cut into long strips, and patted dry

5 tablespoons (1 oz) whole-stem fresh peppercorns

SPICES

3 teaspoons chile powder (optional)

1 teaspoon ground turmeric

PANTRY

About 1 cup (8 oz) sea salt flakes

2 teaspoons light brown sugar

1. Place the lemons, garlic, ginger, and peppercorns in a large bowl and cover with the chile powder, if using, turmeric, salt, and sugar.

2. Using your clean hands, rub in the spices, making sure everything is well coated.

3. Transfer the mixture to a sterilized jar with a tight-fitting lid.

4. Place the jar in direct sunlight for 6–8 days, making sure to shake vigorously every other day. Refrigerate for 4–6 weeks.

NOTE: Be sure to scrub the lemons well before using them. Make sure the garlic and ginger are super dry.

SIX
Yogurts

① ROASTED EGGPLANT

PREHEAT the broiler.

RUB oil over 1 large eggplant, prick all over, and broil for 20 minutes. Turn every 3–4 minutes, or until the skin is scorched and the eggplant is soft. Let cool, then remove the skin and finely chop or mash.

HEAT ½ tablespoon oil in a frying pan. Add ¼ teaspoon cumin seeds, 4–5 fresh curry leaves, ¼ teaspoon ground ginger, and ¼ finely chopped onion and fry over low heat, stirring, for 1–2 minutes. Stir in ¼ teaspoon ground coriander, ¼ teaspoon chile powder, and salt to taste. Fry for 30 seconds. Stir in the eggplant and cook for 6–8 minutes.

REMOVE from the heat, let cool, then place in a bowl and mix in 1½ cups (12 oz) Greek yogurt.

GARNISH with finely chopped cilantro and ½ tablespoon pomegranate seeds, if you like.

② POTATO AND TOASTED CUMIN

BOIL 1 large potato with the skin on, then let cool and chop into small cubes.

TOAST 1 teaspoon cumin seeds, 1 teaspoon pomegranate seeds, and ¼ teaspoon coriander seeds in a nonstick pan over medium-low heat. Let cool, then grind in a mortar and pestle to grind until coarse. Reserve 1 teaspoon for the garnish.

MIX the rest of the spices with the potatoes, 1½ cups (12 oz) plain yogurt, and ¼ teaspoon chaat masala.

SEASON with sea salt and coarse black pepper.

GARNISH with the reserved spice mix and finely chopped cilantro.

③ SPINACH AND MINT

PUT 5–6 mint leaves, a large pinch of dried mint, 1 finely chopped garlic clove, 1 teaspoon toasted cumin seeds, and a large pinch of salt in a mortar and pestle, and grind to make a smooth paste.

PLACE 8 oz cooked chopped spinach into a bowl together with the mint paste and stir in 1 cup (8 oz) plain or Greek yogurt.

GARNISH with ¾-inch piece peeled and grated ginger and finely sliced red chile, if you like.

④ CRISPY OKRA

PLACE 1 cup (8 oz) plain or Greek yogurt in a bowl.

STIR in ¼ teaspoon dried mint, a large pinch of chile powder, ¼ teaspoon chaat masala, and salt to taste.

GARNISH with 2 tablespoons Crispy Okra (page 232) and a large pinch of toasted and finely crushed cumin seeds and toasted sesame seeds, if you like.

⑤ RAW VEGETABLES

CHOP very finely ½ small carrot, ¼ celery rib, ¼ green bell pepper, ¼ red onion.

COMBINE with 1 tablespoon finely chopped cilantro and 1 small seeded tomato in a large bowl.

STIR in 1 cup (8 oz) plain or Greek yogurt, 1 finely crushed garlic clove, ¼ teaspoon ground cumin, and salt to taste.

HEAT 1 teaspoon oil in a pan and fry ½ teaspoon black mustard seeds, ½ finely sliced red chile, and 3–4 fresh curry leaves. Let cool slightly and stir into the yogurt, reserving a little for the garnish.

⑥ CARROT, CUCUMBER, AND CILANTRO

MIX together in a large bowl grated ½ small carrot, grated 2-inch piece seeded cucumber (squeezed dry with a cloth), ¼ minced garlic clove, ¼ finely chopped small green chile, seeded if you like, ¼ teaspoon dried mint, ¼ teaspoon ground cumin, a large pinch of chaat masala (optional), 1 cup (8 oz) plain yogurt, and salt and coarse black pepper to taste.

GARNISH with 1 tablespoon finely chopped Green Onion, Cilantro, and Mint (page 232), if you like.

desserts and drinks

CHAPTER 7

Pistachio Kulfi

THIS IS A QUICK VERSION OF A CLASSIC INDIAN ICE CREAM. REPLACE
SOME OR ALL OF THE PISTACHIOS WITH FINELY CHOPPED DRIED OR
FRESH FRUIT AND OR MIXED NUTS. THE KULFI IS DELICIOUS ON ITS
OWN, OR SERVE WITH GRIDDLED OR GRILLED TROPICAL FRUIT.

SERVES 4 | PREPARATION TIME: 10 MINUTES | FREEZING TIME: AT LEAST 6 HOURS

FRESH

2½ cups heavy or whipping cream

SPICES

2 pinches of saffron threads,
soaked in a little warm milk
(see Saffron Essence, page 228)

2 pinches of green cardamom seeds

1 teaspoon kewra water (optional;
see page 15)

PANTRY

2½ cups condensed milk

2½ cups evaporated milk

2 tablespoons pistachios,
finely chopped

1. In a large bowl, thoroughly mix together the cream, condensed milk, and evaporated milk.

2. Add the soaked saffron with the soaking milk, cardamom seeds, and kewra water, if using, to the milk mixture and mix together.

3. Finally, add most of the chopped pistachios, setting a spoonful aside for decoration, and stir until the mixture is well combined. Pour into a freezerproof container.

4. Freeze for at least 6 hours. Remove 5–10 minutes before serving and decorate with the reserved pistachios.

NOTE: Stir the ice cream once halfway through the freezing time, so the nuts don't settle at the bottom. The kulfi can also be frozen in individual molds.

Almond and Saffron Cake

SUPER MOIST AND FEATHER LIGHT, THIS CAKE HAS BITTER HINTS
OF ORANGE PEEL AND GENTLE POPS OF CARDAMOM.
SERVE AND ENJOY ANY TIME OF THE DAY.

SERVES 8–10 | PREPARATION TIME: 1 HOUR | COOKING TIME: 50–55 MINUTES

FRESH

2 oranges (about 10 oz),
roughly chopped (including peel)

5 eggs, separated

SPICES

Small pinch of ground
cardamom seeds

Pinch of saffron threads,
soaked in warm milk
(see Saffron Essence, page 228

PANTRY

1 cup superfine sugar

2 cups ground almonds

2 tablespoons sliced almonds

2 tablespoons sifted
confectioners' sugar

1. Preheat the oven to 350°F, then line the base and sides of a 9-inch springform cake pan with parchment paper.

2. Heat the oranges in a pan over low heat together with 1 tablespoon water. Cover and cook gently for 30 minutes, or until the oranges are soft and the liquid has evaporated. Remove the pan from the heat and let cool, then finely chop in a high-speed blender or with a knife.

3. Whisk the egg whites in a clean, dry bowl until they form soft peaks. Gradually stir in half the superfine sugar and continue to whisk for 1 minute.

4. Next, in a separate bowl, whisk the egg yolks together with the remaining superfine sugar for 2–3 minutes. Whisk in the oranges, then gently fold in the ground almonds, cardamom seeds, and saffron with the soaking milk. Using a large metal spoon, slowly fold in spoonfuls of the egg whites until everything is well combined.

5. Pour the mixture into the prepared cake pan, sprinkle the sliced almonds over the top, and bake in the oven for 50–55 minutes, or until golden brown, checking every 20 minutes.

6. Leave the cake to cool in the pan before turning out and dusting with the confectioners' sugar. Store the cake in an airtight container for up to 3 days.

Orange and Carrot Balls with Chocolate

THIS IS AN IMPRESSIVE DESSERT, ESPECIALLY IF PILED HIGH LIKE A PYRAMID, DRIZZLED WITH RIPPLES OF HOT DARK CHOCOLATE, AND SCATTERED WITH TOASTED MIXED NUTS. ALTERNATIVELY, SERVE THE HOT CHOCOLATE ON THE SIDE AS A DIP.

SERVES 4–6 | PREPARATION TIME: 30 MINUTES | COOKING TIME: 1½ HOURS

FRESH

1 lb carrots, finely grated

Zest of 1 large orange

3 cups whole milk

SPICES

6–8 green cardamom pods

PANTRY

6 tablespoons very finely chopped almonds

¾ cup superfine sugar

⅓ cup ghee or unsalted butter

1 bar (5 oz) good-quality dark chocolate

2 tablespoons sliced almonds, lightly toasted

2 tablespoons pistachios, lightly toasted

1. Combine the carrots, orange zest, chopped almonds, sugar, and milk in a heavy pan and stir over low heat until the sugar has dissolved. Cook over medium heat for about 1½ hours. The mixture should be stirred from time to time to prevent the carrots from sticking to the bottom. Cook until the mixture thickens and most of the liquid has evaporated. Keep stirring, especially during the later stage of cooking.

2. Using a mortar and pestle or a rolling pin, gently break the cardamom pods and crush the seeds.

3. Melt the ghee in a separate pan and add the crushed cardamom pods and seeds. Stir in the carrot mixture and fry over medium-low heat until the carrot mixture becomes reddish brown.

4. Remove the pan from the heat and let cool. Once the mixture has cooled, pick out the cardamom pods. Take a double teaspoonful of thev mixture and roll into a smooth ball. Repeat until the mixture is used. Arrange the balls on a flat platter or pile high, creating a tall pyramid.

5. Break the chocolate into pieces and put into a heatproof bowl. Place the bowl over a pan of gently simmering water, making sure the bowl does not touch the water, and leave to melt.

6. Using a rolling pin, roughly crush the toasted sliced almonds and pistachios.

7. Liberally drizzle the balls with hot melted chocolate and shower with the toasted sliced almonds and pistachios.

NOTE: It is important that the pan be heavy; otherwise there is a risk of the carrot mixture burning.

Spiced Fruit Salad

HERE'S A SIMPLE AND LIGHT DESSERT, WHICH WOULD BE PERFECT OFFERED
AT THE END OF A RICH MEAL. SERVE ALONGSIDE GOOD-QUALITY ICE CREAM
OR ADD A DROP OF RUM AND GINGER PEELINGS TO THE SUGAR SYRUP.

SERVES 4–5 | PREPARATION TIME: 40 MINUTES
STANDING TIME: 1 HOUR | COOKING TIME: 6–7 MINUTES

FRESH

Zest and juice of 1 lime

Zest and juice of 1 lemon

4 tablespoons blueberries

1 small pineapple, peeled and sliced

1 large mango, finely sliced
or chopped

2 kiwifruits, finely sliced

1 large blood orange, peeled
and cut into segments

5 lychees, halved

½ papaya, finely sliced

2 passion fruits

SPICES

2 cloves

1 star anise

1 cassia or cinnamon stick

1 vanilla pod, split open lengthwise
and seeds scraped out

PANTRY

½ cup superfine sugar

1. Mix together the sugar, ½ cup water, cloves, star anise, cassia, and vanilla pod and seeds in a pan. Simmer gently until the sugar has dissolved, then continue simmering for a further 5–6 minutes.

2. Stir in the lime and lemon zest and juice, then remove the pan from the heat and let cool completely.

3. Meanwhile, put the blueberries, pineapple, mango, kiwifruits, blood orange, lychees, papaya, and passion fruits into a serving dish, then pour or strain the sugar syrup over the fruit. Leave to stand for at least 1 hour before serving.

Pomegranate, Lime, and Rose Water Granita

THIS SEMIFROZEN DESSERT IS SO SIMPLE AND WORKS WELL WITH
MOST FLAVORS—FOR EXAMPLE, TRY WATERMELON, PINEAPPLE, BLOOD ORANGE,
LEMON AND MINT, OR BLUEBERRY. ALTERNATIVELY, ENJOY AS A DRINK—JUST
SCOOP A LARGE SPOONFUL INTO A BEAUTIFUL GLASS, ADD A TEASPOON
OF POMEGRANATE SEEDS, AND TOP UP WITH CHILLED PROSECCO.

SERVES 4 | PREPARATION TIME: 20 MINUTES | FREEZING TIME: 3–4 HOURS

FRESH
1⅔ cups pomegranate juice
½ cup orange juice
Juice of ½ lime

SPICES
1 teaspoon rose water (optional)

PANTRY
¼ cup golden superfine sugar

1. Place the pomegranate and orange juices and sugar in a saucepan and stir over low heat until the sugar is dissolved. Combine with the lime juice and rose water and set aside to cool.

2. Pour the mixture into a metal baking pan. Carefully place in the freezer and freeze until solid, about 2 hours, then whisk with a fork and return to the freezer for a further 1–2 hours. Stir to break up the ice crystals at 1-hour intervals until the granita is light and easy to scoop.

3. Scoop and serve.

NOTE: It's important to freeze the granita in a metal pan, because the metal keeps the mixture colder and at the right consistency.

Creamy Honey and Raisin Vermicelli Pots

THIS IS A RICH AND COMFORTING DESSERT, WHICH CAN BE
EATEN HOT OR COLD AND TAKES ONLY MINUTES TO MAKE.
ENRICH THIS DISH EVEN FURTHER BY SERVING WITH
ROASTED OR STEWED PLUMS, APPLES, OR PEACHES.

SERVES 4 | PREPARATION TIME: 10 MINUTES | COOKING TIME: 8–10 MINUTES

FRESH

2 cups whole milk

Zest of 1 orange

1 tablespoon heavy cream

SPICES

¼ teaspoon ground cardamom seeds

PANTRY

2 tablespoons ghee or unsalted butter

3½–4 oz fine wheat or rice vermicelli,
broken into small- and
medium-size pieces

3–4 tablespoons superfine sugar

1 tablespoon raisins or finely
chopped apricots or dates

DECORATION

1 tablespoon runny honey

1 tablespoon sliced almonds,
lightly toasted

1. Heat the ghee in a heavy pan over medium-low heat.

2. Add the broken vermicelli and stir-fry for about
1 minute, or until golden.

3. Reduce the heat and pour in the milk, sugar, ground
cardamom seeds, raisins, and orange zest. Stir and gently
simmer for 5 minutes, then add the cream and continue
cooking for a further 2–3 minutes, or until it thickens.

4. Turn off the heat, serve in individual pots, and decorate
with honey and sliced almonds.

Masala Chai

To give this blend an extra indulgent touch, add dried rose petals and saffron, or for more earthy flavors, try nutmeg and star anise. For a faster and lighter tea, take a teaspoon of this blend and infuse in a pot of tea, then make it the traditional way with a drop of cold milk.

MAKES 1 CUP | PREPARATION TIME: 15 MINUTES | COOKING TIME: 8–10 MINUTES

SPICES
1 cup (3 oz) fennel seeds
30 green cardamom pods, slightly cracked
1½ teaspoons cloves
1½ cinnamon sticks
3 teaspoons ground ginger
⅔ cup (2 oz) mace

PANTRY
Sugar, to taste

1. Heat a frying pan over medium-low heat and toast the fennel seeds, cardamom, cloves, and cinnamon for 5–7 minutes. Remove from the heat and let cool completely.

2. Place the toasted spices together with the ground ginger and mace in a mortar and pestle and grind to a very coarse powder. Store in an airtight container for up to 2 months.

3. For 1 cup of chai, boil the milk, 6 tablespoons water, 2 teaspoons spice mix, and 1 teabag black tea in a pan over medium heat for 4–5 minutes. Gradually bring to a boil, then reduce the heat and add sugar. Strain and serve.

NOTE: Masala chai and hot samosas make the perfect and most irresistible partnership.

Ayurvedic Jamu Tonic Drink

THIS IS A HIGHLY ANTIOXIDANT AYURVEDIC TONIC THAT CAN
ALSO HELP TO IMPROVE BLOOD CIRCULATION. FOR MAXIMUM BENEFITS,
DRINK WARM OR COLD THROUGHOUT THE DAY.

MAKES 1 QUART | PREPARATION TIME: 1 HOUR

FRESH
Juice of 2 limes

SPICES
¼ cup ground turmeric
or ½ tablespoon fresh root, peeled and
crushed in a blender

PANTRY
1 quart filtered water

1 tablespoon agave syrup
(natural sweetener; optional)

2½ oz dry tamarind

5 tablespoons manuka honey

1. Combine the filtered water, the turmeric, agave syrup, and dry tamarind together in a pan. Bring to a boil and boil for 30 minutes.

2. Remove from the heat, add the lime juice and manuka honey. Stir well and let cool for as long as possible.

3. Once cool, strain into a jug with a lid. Store in the refrigerator for up to 2 days.

Chile Hot Chocolate

THIS QUIRKY, CHILE-SPIKED HOT CHOCOLATE DRINK IS SPICED UP WITH RED PEPPER FLAKES AND INFUSED WITH A WARM SWEETNESS, WHICH COMES FROM THE NUTMEG AND CINNAMON. SERVE WITH SWEET FRUIT BREAD PERFECT FOR DIPPING.

SERVES 4 | PREPARATION TIME: 5 MINUTES
STANDING TIME: 8–10 MINUTES | COOKING TIME: 15 MINUTES

FRESH
3 cups whole milk
5 tablespoons half-and-half

SPICES
1 cinnamon stick
Pinch of grated nutmeg
1 dried red chile

PANTRY
3 tsp drinking chocolate powder
5 oz good-quality dark chocolate, at least 70% cocoa solids, roughly chopped

SERVE
6 tablespoons whipped heavy cream
Grated chocolate
Small pinch of red pepper flakes
Sugar, to taste

1. Heat the milk, cream, cinnamon stick, nutmeg, and chile in a heavy saucepan over medium-high heat. Bring to a boil, then remove from the heat, cover, and set aside for 8–10 minutes to infuse.

2. Strain into a clean pan and reheat over low heat for 2–3 minutes (don't boil).

3. Add the chocolate powder and chopped chocolate, and whisk until smooth and melted.

4. Serve with whipped cream, grated chocolate, and a very small sprinkle of pepper flakes, adding sugar, if you like.

NOTE: If you're making this hot chocolate for children, consider omitting the chile.

Cardamom Coffee

ADD THIS SMOKY AND EARTHY CARDAMOM MILK TO YOUR FAVORITE
GOOD-QUALITY COFFEE AND ENJOY AS AN EARLY MORNING DRINK—OR,
POUR THE CONCOCTION INTO SHOT GLASSES AND SERVE AT THE END
OF A DELICIOUS MEAL. YOU CAN ALSO REPLACE THE CARDAMOM WITH
ANY SPICES YOU DESIRE—CINNAMON, NUTMEG, OR STAR ANISE.

SERVES 1 | PREPARATION TIME: 5 MINUTES | COOKING TIME: 5–6 MINUTES

FRESH
⅔ cup milk

SPICES
5–6 cardamom pods, slightly cracked

PANTRY
5 tablespoons freshly brewed hot coffee of your choice
Sugar, to taste

1. In a saucepan, heat the milk and cardamom pods over medium-low heat for 4–5 minutes, stirring and whisking frequently to create a froth. Leave to stand and infuse.

2. Strain and gently heat when ready to use.

3. Pour the hot coffee into a pot or cup, add sugar, and pour in the spiced milk.

Ayurvedic Detox Tea

THIS SIMPLE CLEANSING TEA HELPS TO NOURISH YOUR BODY,
BOOST YOUR METABOLISM, AND BALANCE YOUR DIGESTIVE SYSTEM.
TRY TO DRINK THIS SPICE-INFUSED WATER THROUGHOUT THE DAY.
ADD A LITTLE HONEY OR APPLE JUICE FOR SWEETNESS.

MAKES 1 QUART | PREPARATION TIME: 5 MINUTES
STANDING TIME: 10–15 MINUTES | COOKING TIME: 10 MINUTES

FRESH
1 quart filtered water
2 thin slices peeled ginger

SPICES
1 teaspoon cumin seeds
5 cloves
½ teaspoon black peppercorns
1 teaspoon fennel seeds
1 teaspoon coriander seeds
1 cinnamon stick

1. Pour the filtered water into a large saucepan, add the ginger and all the spices, and bring to a boil, then reduce the heat and simmer for 5–10 minutes.

2. Turn off the heat. Cover and leave to infuse for 10–15 minutes. Drink hot or cold.

Fresh Lemon and Lime Soda

THE COOLING COMBINATION OF SOUR, SWEET, AND SALTY IN THIS DRINK
WORKS WELL ALONGSIDE FIERY DISHES, BUT IT'S EQUALLY APPEALING
AS A STAND-ALONE DRINK—ADD A SPLASH OF GIN FOR A FURTHER TWIST.

SERVES 6 | PREPARATION TIME: ABOUT 15 MINUTES | STANDING TIME: 10 MINUTES

FRESH
½ cup lime juice (from 6–7 limes)
½ cup lemon juice (from 6–7 lemons)
½ lime, cut into slices
½ lemon, cut into slices

PANTRY
½ teaspoon salt
2 tablespoons superfine sugar
1 liter soda, tonic, or sparkling water

SERVE
Ice cubes

1. In a small jug, mix together the lime juice, lemon juice, salt, and sugar. Leave to stand for 10 minutes, or until the sugar and salt have dissolved. Reserve until ready to serve.

2. Pour a little citrus mixture into each glass, add a lime and lemon slice, then top up with soda, tonic, or sparkling water. Serve with ice cubes.

Salted and Sweet Lassi

LASSI IS A LIGHT AND TRADITIONAL YOGURT-BASED DRINK. IN INDIA, THIS COOLING BLEND OF YOGURT, WATER, SPICES, AND SOMETIMES FRUIT IS A POPULAR BEVERAGE TO HAVE ON SUPER-HOT DAYS OR AS AN ACCOMPANIMENT TO SPICY DISHES. LASSI CAN ALSO BE REFRIGERATED FOR A COUPLE OF HOURS BEFORE SERVING.

SEERVES 2–3 | PREPARATION TIME: 5–10 MINUTES

Salted

FRESH
2½ cups (20 oz) chilled plain yogurt

SPICES
1½ teaspoons toasted cumin seeds, coarsely crushed
1 teaspoon black salt or table salt

PANTRY
7–8 ice cubes, crushed

DECORATION
5–6 mint leaves, finely shredded

1. In a jug, whisk together the yogurt, 1 cup cold water, cumin (reserving a little for the decoration), and salt and mix together until smooth and frothy.

2. Pour into tall glasses, add ice, and decorate with mint and the reserved cumin.

Sweet

FRESH
1½ cups (12 oz) plain yogurt
½ cup cold water or milk

SPICES
Large pinch ground cardamom
Small pinch saffron threads, soaked in a little warm milk (see Saffron Essence, page 228)
1 teaspoon rose water

PANTRY
6 teaspoons sugar
7–8 ice cubes, crushed

DECORATION
1 tablespoon mixed crushed pistachio and blanched almonds

1. In a jug, whisk together the yogurt, ground cardamom (reserving a little for the decoration), saffron, rose water, sugar, and water or milk until smooth and frothy.

2. Pour into glasses, add ice, and decorate with crushed nuts and the reserved ground cardamom.

basics

CHAPTER 8

TAMARIND PULP

MAKES 1 ¼ – 1 ½ CUPS (¾ – 1 LB)
PREPARATION TIME: ABOUT 10 MINUTES
COOKING TIME: 10 – 12 MINUTES

In most North Indian dishes, tomatoes form the main base, but for South Indian dishes, tamarind is the key ingredient, especially for sauce-based dishes. This tart fruit pulp is used to add tang and sourness. It is very versatile and easy to prepare, so make a large amount and use in marinades, dips, and chutneys or rice, vegetable, and fish dishes.

FRESH
8-oz block seedless tamarind

1. Place the tamarind and 1½ cups water together in a pan and simmer gently for 10–12 minutes, or until softened through. Drain through a fine sieve, using the back of a spoon to keep scraping it until you are left with any errant seeds and fibers. When it's cool enough, use your hands to further loosen the pulp.

2. Pour the tamarind pulp into a screw-top jar and refrigerate. Use within 1 month.

SAFFRON ESSENCE

MAKES ABOUT ¼ CUP
PREPARATION TIME: ABOUT 10 MINUTES
SOAKING TIME: 15 – 25 MINUTES

Saffron is a high-quality spice and is the most expensive in the world. A tiny amount of these delicate threads goes a long way. Presoaking your saffron draws out the color and helps to ensure that the flavors infuse evenly throughout the dish.

SPICES
2–3 saffron threads
PANTRY
¼ cup warm cooking liquid, such as milk, water, or stock

1. Immerse the saffron threads in the liquid and soak for 15–25 minutes.

2. Pour the saffron and the liquid into your dish—usually towards the end of the cooking.

Two Essential Pastes

The use of these pastes is paramount in Indian cooking, so it's worth making them in large batches, or prep the pastes 2 days before entertaining, so all the groundwork has been done.

CARAMELIZED ONION PASTE

MAKES 1 LB
PREPARATION TIME: ABOUT 10 MINUTES
COOKING TIME: ABOUT 30 MINUTES

A sweet, silky smooth paste for all onion-based sauces or even marinades, it gives any dish a glossy sleek finish. To make a richer paste, blend with cashew nuts, yogurt, or fried garlic and ginger.

FRESH
1¼ lb onions, finely sliced
PANTRY
4–5 tablespoons oil

1. Heat the oil in a heavy frying pan over medium-low heat. Add the onions and fry, stirring, for 5–8 minutes.

2. Turn up the heat slightly and keep stirring and frying for 15–20 minutes, or until the onions have become rich and golden.

3. Place the caramelized onions in a blender and blitz until smooth.

4. Place the paste in a jar and seal with a tight-fitting lid. Refrigerate for 1 week or place in small containers and freeze.

NOTE: Use a touch of water or more oil only if needed.

GINGER AND GARLIC PASTE

MAKES 4 OZ
PREPARATION TIME: 10–12 MINUTES

A fabulous paste that has endless uses—try in all curries, marinades, dressing, and dips. Prior to blending the ginger and garlic, you can also add a couple of fresh chiles.

FRESH
4-inch piece ginger, peeled and roughly chopped
28 garlic cloves (2–3 heads), roughly chopped

1. Place the ginger and garlic together in a blender or use a mortar and pestle and grind to a fine paste.

2. Place the paste in a jar and seal with a tight-fitting lid. Refrigerate for 3 days or place in small containers and freeze.

NOTE: Top with a little oil if storing for longer than 2 days.

GREEN ONION, CILANTRO, AND MINT

MAKES ABOUT 3 TABLESPOONS
PREPARATION TIME: ABOUT 5 MINUTES

This is refreshing and cleansing. Use to garnish yogurt dishes, meats, chutneys, and salads.

FRESH
3 green onions
¼ bunch cilantro, including stalks
6–7 mint leaves

Very finely shred the green onions, cilantro, and mint, mix together, and use immediately.

NOTE: Mint and cilantro go black if left to stand for too long—if not using straightaway, lightly coat the whole garnish with 1 teaspoon of oil and keep in the refrigerator.

CRISPY OKRA

MAKES 1 LB
PREPARATION TIME: 12–15 MINUTES
COOKING TIME: 3–5 MINUTES

This certainly is a different and interesting way to cook and eat okra. Use to garnish lentils, yogurts, salads, and rice or simply eat as a hot, crispy snack—if so, sprinkle with a pinch of chaat masala while hot.

FRESH
1 lb okra, finely sliced lengthwise
¼ teaspoon lemon juice
SPICES
½ teaspoon garam masala
¼ teaspoon ground turmeric
1 teaspoon chile powder
PANTRY
1 tablespoon cornstarch
¼ teaspoon salt
Oil, for deep-frying

1. Dry the okra carefully. Cut down the middle and then into batons.

2. Place the okra in a bowl and sprinkle with the lemon juice, spices, cornstarch, and salt. Stir and coat evenly, then leave to absorb for 20–25 minutes.

3. Heat the oil for deep-frying in a large, deep saucepan or a wok and deep-fry the okra in batches until golden and crisp. Remove and drain on paper towels. Let cool completely.

HOW TO MAKE
Ghee

GHEE IS A TYPE OF CLARIFIED BUTTER, SIMMERED SLOWLY UNTIL ALL THE MOISTURE EVAPORATES AND THE MILK SOLIDS BEGIN TO BROWN. AS IT IS HEATED FOR LONGER, GHEE DEVELOPS A STRONG, NUTTY, AND CARAMEL-LIKE FLAVOR AND AROMA. AYURVEDIC DEVOTEES CALL GHEE LIQUID GOLD, AS IT HAS MANY HEALTH BENEFITS. IT IS ALSO LACTOSE-INTOLERANT-FRIENDLY AND HAS A HIGH BURNING POINT, SO IT'S PERFECT FOR FRYING. IF YOU PREFER NOT TO COOK WITH GHEE, THEN A FEW TEASPOONS DRIZZLED ON THE FINISHED DISH BEFORE SERVING WILL GIVE IT THAT EXTRA EDGE OF FLAVOR.

MAKES ABOUT 1½ CUPS | PREPARATION TIME: 5 MINUTES | COOKING TIME: 20–25 MINUTES

EQUIPMENT

HEAVY PAN
FINE SIEVE
WOODEN SPOON
SEVERAL PIECES OF CHEESECLOTH
STERILIZED GLASS JAR

cut

melt

check

1

Place 1 lb good-quality butter, cut into small cubes, into the pan.

note For best results use organic butter.

2

Gently start to melt over medium-low heat, stirring constantly. Once it really starts to melt, the butter will separate into 3 layers. This will start to happen quite quickly.

3

Foam will appear on top, milk solids will drop to the bottom, and you should be left with clarified butter floating in between the two. To check, use a spoon to push back the foam and take a look.

simmer

strain

5

Next, place a piece of cheesecloth over a sterilized glass jar and carefully strain to remove the brown toasted milk proteins sitting at the base of the pan. Keep chilled for up to 6 months.

4

Bring the butter to a gentle simmer, turn down the heat, and cook gently for a further 15–20 minutes, or until the middle layer becomes more fragrant and golden than when you first started. Push back the foam to take a look.

With a fine sieve or a spoon, skim and lift off absolutely all the foam sitting on top and discard. All that should be left is the clear butter and brown milk solids sitting at the bottom. Turn up the heat slightly and brown just a little more. Then turn off the heat and allow the ghee to settle for 1–2 minutes.

Ghee

store

Concentrated Spice Pastes

PREPARE THESE PASTES 3–4 DAYS IN ADVANCE. PLACE IN A JAR, TOP WITH
A LITTLE OIL, AND REFRIGERATE. YOU CAN PLAY AROUND WITH A LITTLE
AMOUNT OF THE PASTE IN DIPS, MARINADES, DRESSINGS, AND WITH RICE
OR USE TO MAKE A SUBSTANTIAL MEAT, VEGETABLE, OR PANEER DISH.

SAFFRON AND CARDAMOM PASTE

MAKES ABOUT 1 CUP
PREPARATION TIME: ABOUT 30 MINUTES
COOKING TIME: 12–15 MINUTES

Having this in your pantry makes it easy to plan ahead for any occasion, or to use as an everyday condiment in other recipes.

FRESH
8 oz onions, sliced and fried until golden and crispy
3–4 garlic cloves

SPICES
Seeds from 15 green cardamom pods

1 tablespoon white poppy seeds and 2–3 saffron threads, soaked in ½ cup hot water for 15 minutes

1 tablespoon garam masala

PANTRY
3 tablespoons oil, or as needed
Salt, to taste

1. Using a mortar and pestle, grind the cardamom pods and poppy seeds together, then place all the ingredients in a blender and grind into a smooth paste. Add a little extra oil if needed.

2. Place in a sterilized jar, seal with a tight-fitting lid, and refrigerate for up to 6 days.

NOTE: Empty the whole jar into a heavy pan, fry for 30 seconds over medium heat, then add ¼ teaspoon ground turmeric, 2 teaspoons ground cumin, 1 teaspoon red pepper flakes, then meat, paneer, or vegetables of your choice, and add ¼ cup water. Cover and slow cook. Finish with some shredded ginger and crème fraîche or coconut milk for additional flavor.

BASIC SPICED TOMATO PASTE

MAKES ABOUT 1 ½ CUPS
PREPARATION TIME: ABOUT 15 MINUTES
COOKING TIME: ABOUT 30 MINUTES

It's worthwhile making a large batch, as this paste is the perfect all-rounder and base for almost all Indian curries and rice dishes. No more buying jars of spice paste from supermarkets; this fresh and authentic one beats them all.

FRESH
8 oz onions
3–4 garlic cloves
1-inch piece ginger, peeled
2–3 green chiles
8 oz tomatoes, finely diced
SPICES
3 bay leaves
3 black cardamom pods, seeds removed
1 cassia or cinnamon stick
2 tablespoons coriander seeds
3 cloves
1 teaspoon ground turmeric
PANTRY
3 tablespoons oil
Salt, to taste

1. In a blender, grind the onions, garlic, ginger, and chiles together to form a paste. Set aside.

2. In a coffee/spice grinder or blender, grind the bay leaves, black cardamom, cassia, coriander seeds, and cloves. Set aside.

3. Heat the oil in a heavy frying pan over medium-high heat. Add the onion paste and fry, stirring frequently, for 5–7 minutes, or until it is a rich golden brown.

4. Turn the heat down slightly, add the turmeric and salt, and fry for 30 seconds.

5. Next, add the tomatoes and cook until the tomatoes break down and any water has evaporated. At this stage, blitz in a blender again for an even smoother paste, if you like.

6. Add the spice powder and stir together well.

7. Place the paste in a sterilized jar, seal with a tight-fitting lid, and refrigerate for up to 6 days.

Toppings and Garnishes

THESE FEW ESSENTIAL INGREDIENTS CAN ADD A LITTLE
EXTRA BOOST, DRAMA, AND FLAVOR TO MOST DISHES.

CRISPY GINGER, ONION, AND GARLIC

MAKES 4–5 TABLESPOONS
PREPARATION TIME: ABOUT 5 MINUTES
COOKING TIME: 10–12 MINUTES

Use this smoky charred garlic and ginger with sweet
caramelized onions to garnish lentils, vegetables,
meats, and any rice dish.

FRESH
2 onions, finely sliced
4 garlic cloves, finely sliced
½-inch piece ginger, peeled and finely shredded
PANTRY
2–3 tablespoons oil
Pinch of salt, or to taste

1. Heat the oil in a frying pan over medium-low
heat. Add the onions and salt, cover, and cook
for 2 minutes.

2. Remove the lid, turn up the heat slightly, and add
the garlic and ginger. Fry, stirring occasionally, for
5–8 minutes, or until crisp, golden, and slightly singed.

NOTE: Fry very slowly for intense flavors.

TOASTED COCONUT, POMEGRANATE SEEDS, AND CILANTRO

MAKES 2–3 TABLESPOONS
PREPARATION TIME: ABOUT 10 MINUTES

This has a nutty, sour, and fresh flavor. Use to
garnish salads, rice, and dry vegetable dishes.

FRESH
Seeds from ½ fresh pomegranate
2 tablespoons finely chopped cilantro
PANTRY
1⅓ cup (4 oz) desiccated coconut

1. Gently toast the coconut in a nonstick pan
over low heat until golden brown, then remove
and let cool.

2. Mix the coconut together with the pomegranate
seeds and cilantro.

CURRY LEAVES, GARLIC, GINGER, AND RED CHILE

MAKES 5–6 TABLESPOONS
PREPARATION TIME: 8–10 MINUTES
COOKING TIME: 2–4 MINUTES

This adds an amazing South Indian flavor and heat to any dish. Use to garnish lentil-based dishes, rice, or charred and roasted vegetables.

FRESH
8 fresh curry leaves
2-inch piece ginger, peeled and cut into julienne
3–4 garlic cloves, very finely sliced
1 whole large red or green chile, seeded if you like and very finely sliced

PANTRY
2 tablespoons oil

1. Heat the oil in a small frying pan over a medium-low heat.

2. Add the curry leaves, then the ginger and fry for 20 seconds. Lower the heat slightly and add the garlic and chile. Fry until crisp, golden, and slightly singed.

MIXED NUTS AND SEEDS

MAKES: 5–6 TABLESPOONS
PREPARATION TIME: ABOUT 10 MINUTES
COOKING TIME: 4–6 MINUTES

This is ideal for that extra crunch and nutty flavor. Use to garnish salads, dips, rice, and some desserts.

PANTRY
½ cup raw cashews
½ cup raw peanuts
1 tablespoon sunflower seeds
½ tablespoon sesame seeds

1. Preheat the oven to 325°F.

2. Spread the cashews and peanuts on a baking sheet and roast in the oven for 3–4 minutes, then add the seeds. Keep tossing and roast for a further 1–2 minutes.

3. Let cool completely, then coarsely crush using a rolling pin or mortar and pestle.

NOTE: Keep a close eye while toasting—once the nuts and seeds go brown, they can burn very quickly.

Dry Spice Mix

IT'S HANDY HAVING READY-MIXED SPICES. HERE ARE TWO WONDERFUL RECIPES.
ONE, A STRIPPED-BACK CLASSIC FOR CURRIES AND ALL-AROUND USE, AND THE
OTHER MORE SPECIFIC IN FLAVOR TO STIR INTO YOGURT OR CRÈME FRAÎCHE
AND USE AS A MARINADE, OR ADD AT THE TAIL END OF COOKING.

KORMA MASALA

MAKES 2–3 TABLESPOONS
PREPARATION TIME: 5–8 MINUTES

Save this one for special occasions. Mix in with
cream, yogurt, or ghee, or rub or marinate meat
and vegetables, then roast or grill.

SPICES

8 large dried chiles, dry-roasted in a pan
over gentle heat
Seeds of 8 green cardamom pods
2 cinnamon sticks
1 teaspoon ground turmeric
6 cloves
1 teaspoon ground ginger
3 saffron threads

Use a mortar and pestle to grind all the ingredients
into a fine powder.

NOTE: Use only the tiny black seeds of the
cardamom, not the green husks.

SIMPLE GARAM MASALA

MAKES 2 TABLESPOONS
PREPARATION TIME: 5–8 MINUTES

Garam masala is the main spice mix used in almost
all Indian dishes. This is an easy version to start with.
Next, you can add additional whole spices and even
toast them in the oven before grinding.

SPICES

1 teaspoon black peppercorns
1 teaspoon cloves
2-inch piece cassia or cinnamon stick
Seeds of 20 green cardamom pods
Seeds of 2–3 black cardamom pods
1 teaspoon cumin seeds

Use a mortar and pestle to grind all the ingredients
into a powder. Place the mixture in a jar with a tight-
fitting lid and use within a month.

NOTE: Take the seeds from the cardamom, then use
a mortar and pestle to grind into a fine powder.

Marinades

TIKKA MASALA

FOR CHICKEN, LAMB, PANEER, AND VEGETABLES

A rich and aromatic yet mellow marinade—it's best used on roasted or grilled chicken, eggplant, potatoes, and cauliflower.

SERVES 4
PREPARATION TIME: 20 MINUTES

FRESH

1½ cups (12 oz) full-fat yogurt, preferably Greek style

3 garlic cloves

2-inch piece ginger, peeled

1 green chile

SPICES

1 teaspoon garam masala

½ teaspoon ajwain seeds

½ teaspoon tandoori masala

½ teaspoon chile powder

2–3 saffron threads (see Saffron Essence, page 228)

PANTRY

½ tablespoon white vinegar or lemon juice

½ teaspoon salt, or to taste

1 egg white

1 tablespoon oil

1. Pour the yogurt into a large bowl.

2. In a blender, blitz the garlic, ginger, and chile together into a fine paste. Add to the yogurt together with the rest of the ingredients, except the egg white and oil, as these need to be added just before cooking.

SPICED COCONUT AND CRÈME FRAÎCHE

FOR FISH, CHICKEN, AND VEGETABLES

This marinade is best smeared over salmon steaks, a whole chicken, or baby eggplants sliced in half and all roasted. Flake or slice any leftover salmon, chicken, or eggplant, mix with good-quality mayonnaise or just a drizzle of oil, squeeze a lime or lemon over, then finish off with finely chopped green onions and cilantro and season with coarse black pepper and sea salt. Now you have an excellent "next day" sandwich filler.

SERVES 2–3
PREPARATION TIME: 10–15 MINUTES

FRESH

1½ garlic cloves

2 tablespoons crème fraîche

SPICES

1 teaspoon chile powder

½ teaspoon garam masala

¼ teaspoon ground turmeric

¼ teaspoon ground black pepper

¼ teaspoon ground cumin

PANTRY

¼ teaspoon salt, or to taste

1½ tablespoons coconut milk powder

1½ tablespoons oil

1. Begin by pounding the garlic and salt together in a mortar and pestle. Next, add all the spices and coconut milk powder to the crushed garlic and salt paste and pound together gently.

2. Slowly drizzle in the oil and stir in until the marinade comes together and makes a thick paste.

3. Finally, stir in the crème fraîche and use immediately. Alternatively, omit the crème fraîche and pour into a screw-top jar and refrigerate. Use within 2 days. Stir in the crème fraîche when ready to use.

MINT, CILANTRO, GINGER, AND LEMON

FOR CHICKEN AND POTATOES

Rub this marinade all over pieces of chicken or a whole bird, then cover and marinate for 2–3 hours. To add a little richness and creaminess, stir in 2 tablespoons of crème fraîche or plain yogurt to the marinade.

SERVES 4
PREPARATION TIME: 20 MINUTES

FRESH

½ bunch cilantro

10–12 mint leaves

1½-inch piece ginger, peeled

3 garlic cloves

Zest and juice of ½ lemon

1½ green chiles

PANTRY

1 teaspoon salt, or to taste

1 tablespoon oil

1. Blitz all the ingredients except the oil together in a small blender. Gradually add the oil to form a paste.

2. Pour the marinade into a screw-top jar, refrigerate, and use within 2 days.

COCONUT AND TAMARIND WITH RED CHILE AND GROUND SPICES

FOR SEAFOOD

Marinate a whole fish in the marinade, then simply fry strips of onions garlic, and ginger. Pop the fish (including the marinade) into the pan and fry until cooked. Alternatively, roast or grill with wedges of lime.

SERVES 4–6
PREPARATION TIME: 15 MINUTES

FRESH
5 tablespoons Tamarind Pulp (page 228)
1 cup (8 oz) coconut milk

SPICES
5 dried red chiles
2 tablespoons ground coriander
1 tablespoon garam masala
1½ teaspoons ground turmeric

PANTRY
½ teaspoon salt, or to taste
3 tablespoons coconut milk powder

1. Use a mortar and pestle to pound the dried chiles with 1–2 tablespoons hot water into a coarse paste.

2. Mix this red chile paste with the tamarind pulp, ground coriander, garam masala, turmeric, and salt. Add the coconut milk powder and coconut milk and mix well.

3. Pour the marinade into a screw-top jar, refrigerate, and use within 2 days.

TAMARIND, GINGER, AND CHILE

FOR SEAFOOD AND MEAT

Rub this sour and aromatic marinade all over your choice of meat and marinate for at least a couple of hours before cooking. For a looser marinade, stir in 4–5 tablespoons coconut milk, plus a large pinch of sugar, which will also help if it's too tart.

SERVES 4
PREPARATION TIME: 35 MINUTES

FRESH
4-inch piece ginger, peeled and roughly chopped
2–3 chiles, roughly chopped
2 tablespoons Tamarind Pulp (page 228)

SPICES
2 teaspoons coriander seeds
1 teaspoon mustard seeds
1 teaspoon garam masala

PANTRY
1 teaspoon salt, or to taste
1 tablespoon oil

1. Heat a nonstick pan over low heat. Toast and toss the coriander and mustard seeds for 30–40 seconds. Let cool and grind to a powder using a mortar and pestle. Set aside.

2. Next, in a mortar and pestle or blender, grind together the ginger, chiles, and 2 teaspoons hot water.

3. Add the tamarind, toasted spices, garam masala, salt, and oil and mix thoroughly.

4. Pour the marinade into a screw-top jar, refrigerate, and use within 2 days.

SPICED YOGURT

FOR CHICKEN AND MEAT

This marinade is delicious rubbed into a piece of chicken, a steak, or a lamb chop. Stir into mixed vegetables and roast—the marinade creates its own dressing. Any cooked leftovers can be finely sliced and enjoyed as part of a salad or filled in any bread of your choice.

SERVES 4
PREPARATION TIME: 20 MINUTES

FRESH
2 cups (16 oz) plain yogurt
2 garlic cloves, finely crushed
1-inch piece ginger, peeled and finely grated

SPICES
1 tablespoon garam masala
¼ teaspoon ground turmeric

PANTRY
3 tablespoons oil
Salt and coarse black pepper, to taste

1. Stir all the ingredients together.

2. Pour the marinade into a jar with a tight-fitting lid, refrigerate, and use within 2 days.

Bouquet Garni

As aromatic and essential as whole spices are, not many people appreciate randomly biting into them. These little cheesecloth bundles help control and keep track of whole mixed spices without compromising on their flavor. Cut medium-sized squares of cheesecloth, spread out on a work surface, and place the spices in the center. Bring the four corners together and tie them securely with a medium length of kitchen string making sure there are no gaps. Use in any rice, stock, soup, or most sauce-based dishes. Try adding lemon, lime, or orange peels to them.

EIGHT WHOLE SPICE

4–5 whole black peppercorns
1 bay leaf
2–3 cloves
2–3 green cardamom pods, slightly cracked
1 black cardamom pod, slightly cracked
2 single strands of mace
1 small star anise
1-inch cinnamon stick

FIVE WHOLE SPICE

4 small green cardamom pods, slightly cracked
1 teaspoon fennel seeds
4 cloves
2-inch cinnamon stick
¼ teaspoon black peppercorns

THREE WHOLE SPICE

1-inch cassia or cinnamon stick
2 bay leaves
1 teaspoon fennel seeds

FOUR WHOLE SPICE

2 cloves
1 black cardamom pod or 3 small green cardamom pods, slightly cracked
2-inch cassia or cinnamon stick
1 bay leaf

Rich Indian Pastry

This traditional North Indian pastry—flaky and buttery with lots of flavor—is a favorite and base for most Indian street snacks. If there's any pastry left over, roll it out wafer thin, cut into strips or shapes of your choice, sprinkle with mixed seeds such as sesame, caraway, nigella, or black poppy seeds, and deep-fry in batches. Drain and sprinkle with a spice mix of equal amounts of chile powder, sea salt, and sugar. Alternatively, add the same seeds to the dough prior to kneading with water.

MAKES 20–25 SAMOSAS OR PASTIES | PREPARATION TIME: 20 MINUTES

FRESH

1 cup melted butter

1½ teaspoons lemon juice

PANTRY

3 cups (1 lb) all-purpose flour, sifted

Large pinch of salt

1. Combine the flour and salt in a bowl, pour in the butter and lemon juice, and mix together until crumbly.

2. Using your fingertips, bind the ingredients together to form a ball, gradually adding a little warm water if necessary to bring it together into a smooth, pliable dough. Cover with a damp cloth and leave for 20 minutes.

Menu Ideas

LATE BREAKFAST AND BRUNCH: Creamy Peas and Mushrooms (pg. 64); Masala Scrambled Eggs (pg. 70); Carrot and Chickpea Pancakes (pg. 26); Fish, Green Beans, and Spinach Kedgeree (pg. 22); Cardamom Coffee (pg. 218)

SUNDAY LUNCH: Garlic, Ginger, and Chile Prawns (pg. 38); Lemon and Saffron Pot Roast Chicken (pg. 102); Crushed Potatoes (pg. 156); Eggplant with Chile and Pomegranate Dressing (pg. 86); Spiced Fruit Salad (pg. 206)

AFTERNOON CHAI: Spinach and Paneer Samosa (pg. 52); Nargisi Egg Kofta (pg. 70); Tomato, Date, and Tamarind Relish (pg. 176); Almond and Saffron Cake (pg. 202); Masala Chai (pg. 212)

WEEKDAY FAMILY DINNER: Chicken Pulao (pg. 152); Fresh Tomato and Curry Leaf (pg. 88); Kale, Chickpea, Mint, and Preserved Lemon Salad (pg. 162); Cucumber, Carrot, and Mint Chutney (pg. 182); Chile Hot Chocolate (pg. 216)

VEGETARIAN AFFAIR: Tarka Dhal with Spinach and Fresh Tomato (pg. 60); Shallots with Tamarind and Toasted Coconut (pg. 62); Shredded Raw Veg Salad with Spice Dressing and Nuts (pg. 160); Simple Plain Rice (pg. 134); South Indian Eggplant Pickle (p.184)

KIDS: Vegetable Parantha Rolls (pg. 28); Spiced Eggy Bread (pg. 70); Chicken Tikka Wraps (pg. 48); Spicy Sweet-Potato Wedges (pg. 156); Pistachio Kulfi (pg. 200)

SUMMER SUPPER: Salmon Baked with Crème Fraîche and Coconut (pg. 104); Steamed Green Beans in Tomato and Mustard Dressing (pg. 74); Avocado, Corn, Chile, and Cilantro Salad (pg. 166); Fresh Lemon and Lime Soda (pg. 222); Pomegranate, Lime, and Rose Water Granita (pg. 208)

CASUAL DRINKS GATHERING: Squid with Shallots, Ginger, and Chile (pg. 92); Sesame and Ginger Chicken Skewers (pg. 40); Fish Fritters (pg. 34); Paneer and Roasted Red Pepper Filo Cigars (pg. 44); Creamy Honey and Raisin Vermicelli Pots (pg. 210)

Index

ACKNOWLEDGMENTS

I WOULD LIKE TO START by thanking Catie Ziller for not only commissioning me to write this book, but for believing in my ethos and direction. Hopefully this project will not only ignite an interest towards cooking traditional favorites using Indian spices, but also inspire and encourage readers to take each spice further and be more inventive with a more relaxed attitude.

FROM beginning to end I have been thrilled to be able to work with my most perfect and dedicated "dream team." It has been mind-blowing to see the contents of my head come to life.

THANK YOU, Lisa, your unstoppable energy is infectious, you have been so passionate and uplifting to watch—the pictures are simply stunning.

THEN, Aya, for being cool, calm, and collected, your fresh and natural approach has truly given each dish the platform it deserves.

THE backbone of Team India, Rashna, for executing each page from front to back with your graceful and extremely beautiful designs and vision—so inspiring.

ALICE CHADWICK, your wispy line drawings give this book an extra edge that ties the whole thing together and adds a wonderful charm.

LOVELY KATHY, thank you for your patience and support during editing. It has been reassuring to know you were there.

MY TWO GORGEOUS GIRLS, Amaya Lila and Zita Rose, who have been patient, loving, and always believe I can do anything. Love you both X. Also a huge and special thank you to family and friends on whom I have leant for serious support and advice along this journey—I am eternally grateful.

LASTLY, I would like to say a very special and emotional thank you to my parents, Harbhajan Singh Uppal and Sukhbinder Kaur Uppal, for without them I would know nothing. My mother, especially for her handheld teachings of traditional North Indian cuisine, and my father, for constantly inspiring me with his flamboyant, unique, and innovative take on the "spice box" and its execution. All those endless dinner parties and experimenting in the kitchen have paid off. Both your inputs have been truly priceless.

AMANDIP UPPAL

AMANDIP learned how to cook at the age of seven thanks to her Mum, who taught her traditional North Indian dishes, while her gifted father—who's an innovative cook, fearless and borderless when it comes to blending flavors and techniques—taught her to swing out and not get distracted too much by writing things down, but to trust and connect by her sight and smell.

A former stylist and writer, Amandip worked for many years at *The Times* newspaper and magazine, and later went on to become the Deputy Fashion Editor of *Condé Nast Traveller*. Amandip's lifelong love for and interest in food and design inspired her to launch The Lotus Food and Events Company, where she has combined uniquely designed events with her love of food.

Drawing upon all her experiences and love of lifestyle, design, and food, Amandip has created Chile Hot Chocolate—an online kitchen and dining shopping emporium, combining and showcasing her vision and creativity.

weldon**owen**

Published in North America by Weldon Owen, Inc.
1045 Sansome Street, Suite 100
San Francisco, CA 94111
www.weldonowen.com

Weldon Owen is a division of Bonnier Publishing USA

Copyright 2015 © by Marabout

The rights of Amandip Uppal to be identified as author of this book have been asserted in accordance with the Copyright, Design and Patents Act 1988.

Originally published as *My First Indian Kitchen*
First published by Hachette Livre – Marabout
© Hachette Livre – département Marabout

All rights reserved, including the right of reproduction in whole or in part in any form.

Library of Congress Cataloging in Publication data is available.

This edition printed in 2016
10 9 8 7 6 5 4 3 2 1

ISBN 13: 978-1-68188-117-1
ISBN 10: 1-68188-117-9

Printed and bound in China